SONY A9 III

CAMERA

PHOTOGRAPHY

A basic approach to the new Sony Alpha 9 iii camera with
tips on different shooting scenes, and how to focus

Israel Wealth

Contents

INTRODUCTION

The A9 iii is the newest model in the high-speed camera series that introduced Stacked CMOS sensor tech into mirrorless cameras. With its fully global shutter, which reads out all of its pixels at once, the recently released version is the very first full-frame camera to provide such a feature.

This indicates that because the sensor can accomplish all of the functions of mechanical shutter and more, the a9 III doesn't require one. Of its flagship features, this is just a tip of the iceberg.

Nonetheless, this handbook is a beginner guide for users, to master how to focus with the camera, understand some camera terminologies, situations where they apply, how to shoot subjects under different shooting scenes, lens and the different types, vital tips for your perfection, and more.

Get started with your camera.

BASIC KNOWLEDGE

Focal Length

Focal length refers to the distance between the middle of a lens and its focal plane (image sensor), and every lens has varying focal lengths.

Focal length plays a crucial role in lenses since it determines the viewing angle (the scene range that can be captured). As displayed in the pictures below, viewing angle increases with decrease in focal length whereas longer focal length causes distant objects to appear larger.

Notes: The correlation between viewing angle and focal length differs by camera. Unless indicated otherwise, the details within this Shooting Guide are based on the APS-C formats cameras.

11 mm

16 mm

23 mm

33 mm

57 mm

90 mm

200 mm   330 mm

Generally, lenses that have focal lengths of about 35mm are known as **normal lenses**, since their viewing angle is close to that of human visual fields. Lenses with focal lengths less than this are known as **wide-angle lenses**, whereas those with longer focal lengths are known as **telephoto lenses**. Nevertheless, these terms aren't held to strict standards. Different lenses should be used in accordance with the images or subject to be shot.

Shot with a wide-angle lens
Focal length: 11 mm

Shot with a telephoto lens
Focal length: 250 mm

Let us check out your lens' focal length. The range of available focal lengths with that lens is drawn on its body. For instance, focal lengths ranging from 55mm to 200mm can be accessed using **SAL55200-2** in   the   image   below. Likewise, close to the body of the camera (the mount end of the lens barrel), you'll see a marking for the presently set focal length. In the image picture, 55mm is the present focal length.

In this image, **55-200** at the left end indicates the ranges of available focal lengths on the lens. The white markings towards the right end indicates the presently set focal length.

Fixed focal lengths lenses and zoom lenses

Lenses are split into two kinds: **fixed focal lengths lenses**, whose focal lengths are fixed, and **zoom lenses**, whose focal lengths are variable. Certain zoom lenses can be so versatile that they can range from wide-angle to telephoto all by themselves. Alongside being relevant to day-to-day shootings, the lenses are particularly easy for travels whenever you want to minimize your baggage.

Focal length: 20 mm   Focal length: 250 mm

In another scenario, if fixed focal lengths lenses are used, which lack zoom features, you'll need to move to be able to affect its composition. Nevertheless, a fixed focal length lens is normally faster and has wider apertures. They are advantageous in expressions that involve defocused backgrounds and are also able to make use of high-shutter speeds in situations with low-lighting, minimizing image blur. Additionally, they offer superior rendering performances, to enable you enjoy high image-quality that cannot be gotten with zoom lenses.

This picture was captured with fixed focal lengths lenses. When you set small f-numbers as the aperture, it defocuses the background to a huge extent.

Macro lenses, that let you capture close-ups by closing the distance between you and your subject, are likewise fixed focal lengths lenses. Although majority of recent zoom lenses are fitted with macro features that have really small short focusing distances, they are unable to perform exactly like dedicated macro lenses.

Lens: SAL50F18 / Focal length: 50 mm / F-number: 2.0

This picture captured details of sunflowers using macro lenses. With macro lenses, you can get as close as this with your subjects.

Lens: SAL100M28 / Focal length: 100 mm / F-number: 3.5

Learn about lighting and the effect it creates on your shot

Even though you are capturing one particular subject, the impressions your pictures give off are greatly influenced by the lighting. This happens because the intensity and angle of light affects exposure as well as how it creates shadows. Let us check out how combining the subject's position and the light's angle makes any difference.

There are three types of light angles.

  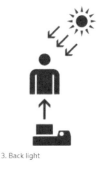

1. Front light   2. Side light   3. Back light

1. Front light

This light illuminates' subjects from the camera side (the front). Since the subjects are exposed directly to light, their shapes and colors are precisely and clearly rendered. This particular lighting is ideal for capturing landscapes, rendering trees and blue skies vividly.

Shot with front light

2. Side light

This light illuminates' subjects from their side. This lighting has a tendency of casting clear shadows on subjects, creating strong contrasts between dark and light. It is most ideal for generating depths through the application of shadows on subjects.

Shot with side light

3. Back light

This light illuminates' subjects from behind. When the back light is used in shooting, it can be used to make food photographs look very appealing or give soft atmospheres to portraits. In another scenario, since strong light filters into the lens, subjects have the tendency to be darker. When this happens, exposure compensation can be used to modify the subject's brightness to your taste.

Shot with back light

When you understand how lighting affects the rendering of subjects, you'll be able to capture photographs that appear how you want them.

For instance, whenever you shoot pictures indoors on sunny days, you can use the light that comes in from the windows. When you stand backing the window, front light can be used in shooting. If the camera is pointing towards the window, the back light can be used in shooting. To capture flowers or foods indoors, it is recommended that you use back light.

Factors affecting Defocus

Interchangeable lenses digital camera with large sensors enables you to freely enjoy defocus renderings unlike other cameras. When you defocus the foreground and background of subjects, subjects appear more impressive.

To regulate the degree of defocus, there are four crucial factors: **distance to a background**, **focusing distance**, **focal length**, and **f-number (aperture)**. You can generate defocus to your desire by effectively combining the above factors.

1. F-number: Reduce this to increase defocus.
2. Focal length: Extend this to increase defocus.
3. Focusing distance: Reduce this to increase defocus.
4. Distance to a background: Increase this to increase defocus.

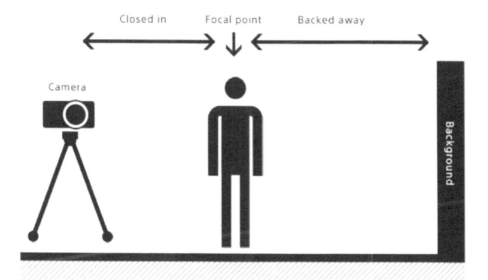

1. The f-number in Aperture

f-number represents the status of aperture. The lower the f-number, the bigger the degree of defocus. The higher the f-number, the lower the degree of defocus.

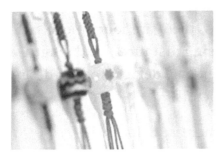

F-number: 2.8

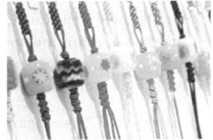

F-number: 16

These pictures were captured from one exact position while only changing the settings of the f-number. With F2.8, the background and foreground are defocused whereas the focal points are on red glass beads. With F16, focal points on the red beads, alongside those behind and in front, are clearly displayed without getting defocused.

2. Focal length

Focal length likewise affects the degree of defocus. Defocus gets larger with longer focal lengths and smaller with shorter focal lengths. When using zoom lenses, the degree of defocus can be increased by shooting with the telephoto end.

Focal length: 35 mm   Focal length: 250 mm

The pictures above were captured using one particular zoom lens, set at 250mm (telephoto side) and 35mm (wide side) respectively. The photographer changed the position of the camera such that the flowers in the foreground are displayed in a particular size in the two pictures. Just like with this example, when there's sufficient space for moving around, the background can be greatly defocused by moving some distance from a subject and capturing using the telephoto end.

3. Focusing distances (the distance between a subject and the camera)

This refers to the extent of defocus changes that are based on camera settings, like **focal length** and **aperture**, as well as on the distance in between the subject and the camera. Background defocus heightens as the camera gets closer to a subject. However, there's a limit to how close you're allowed to move towards a subject.

The pictures below were captured while only changing focusing distance. Picture [1] was captured at 150cm from the subject. In comparison, larger areas of images, except in-focus areas, are defocused in picture [2], and captured about 50cm away.

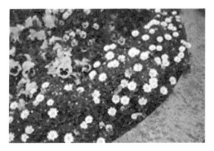

[1] Shot from 150 cm away from the subject

[2] Shot from 50 cm away from the subject

4. Distance between subjects and their backgrounds

The distance in between subjects and their backgrounds as well as between subjects and the camera affects the degree of defocus. The farther a subject is from the background, the more defocused it is. In the pictures below, lenses at the right end were moved backwards to various positions to contrast the degree of defocus.

Both lenses are located at the same distance from the camera.

The lens on the right side is moved back about 15 cm.

The lens on the right side is moved back about 30 cm.

Both lenses can be found at an exact distance from your camera. Lenses at the right end are moved backwards about 15cm. Lenses at the right end are moved backwards about 30cm.

Focus is affixed on lenses at the left end. You can tell that backgrounds are more defocused the farther they get from their focal points (where subjects are located). In instances where background subjects can be moved (for example, when capturing small objects on a table), the extent of defocus can be adjusted to your desire by moving background subjects and the main subjects.

So, the degree of defocus is influenced by four factors; however, you don't need all these factors to generate defocus. Adjust every factor to effectively get defocus based on the shooting conditions.

Minimum/Least Focusing Distances

Every lens has its minimal distance from where subjects can be shot. That distance is known as minimum focusing distances. When you get very close to subjects beyond this distance, you'll be unable to properly focus on them.

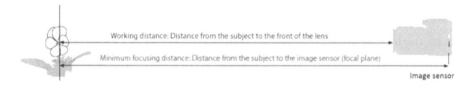

Minimum focusing distances differs by lens; with zoom lenses, focal lengths also causes them to vary. To find out a lens' minimum focusing distances, check the specifications of the lens or check out the distance written on that lens, as displayed in the image below.

The distances are printed at the front end of a lens in feet (ft) and meters (m). The SELP1650 lens displayed above has minimum focusing distances ranging from 25cm (0.25m) through 30cm (0.30m), based on focal length. When you get very close to subjects beyond this distance, you'll be unable to properly focus on subjects, and also be unable to release the shutter.

In instances where you'll need to get very close to subjects (for example, when capturing closeups of flowers), you must first get very close to your subjects. Afterwards begin to move away gradually till you get a distance where subjects are in focus.

Exposure compensation and Exposure

Exposure refers to the quantity of light entering the camera whenever you're shooting photographs. The quantity of light can be ascertained by the shutter speed and aperture. These, alongside ISO sensitivity, determines how bright photographs turn out.

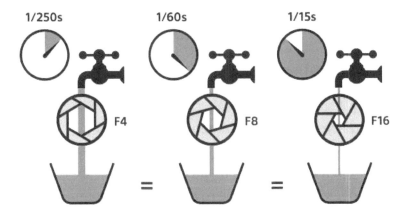

With auto and **P/A/S** shooting modes, the AE (automatic exposure) function is enabled. Due to this, the camera determines optimal exposures and sets ISO sensitivity, shutter speed, and aperture accordingly. When you use the AE function, photographs can be captured with suitable brightness, automatically selected by your camera.

However, based on the circumstances, the brightness determined by your camera to be suitable might be different from your expectations. In pictures captured using the AE feature below, exposure depends on the intermediary brightness in between that dark building and a bright cloud. Nevertheless, to lay emphasis on towering clouds, the darker picture is ideal. In the same vein, in order to clearly render the building, the brighter picture is ideal.

Exposure compensation: +0.7   Exposure compensation: 0   Exposure compensation: -0.7

Exposure compensation: +0.7 Exposure compensation: 0 Exposure compensation: -0.7

In such instances, it is recommended that you use exposure compensation.

Exposure compensation refers to modifications to exposure that your camera deems to be suitable to cause it to look more like your desired brightness. As seen from the example above, the suitable brightness of any picture differs in accordance with your personal tastes or the scene. To increase its brightness, adjust it towards the + end, and to make it darker, slide it towards the - side. With digital cameras, the result of shots can be checked immediately after taking the pictures. Repeatedly make exposure compensation to get your preferred brightness.

A-Mode and Aperture (F-number)

The aperture refers to the part that regulates the quantity of light entering lenses. As displayed in the images below, it's located within the lens, and regulates the quantity of light coming in by altering the dimensions of the openings.

F1.8

F16

The degree of light entering the camera influenced by the sizes of the apertures are referred to as f-numbers. F-numbers have constant standard values, like F8, F5.6, F4, F2.8, and F2. As f-numbers get bigger, aperture closes and minimal light enters the lens.

As f-numbers get smaller, aperture opens and more light gets into the lens. For instance, if aperture changes from F8 to F5.6, it doubles the quantity of light. Due to this, even though you double shutter speed, it allows similar quantity of light into your camera, inasmuch as you leave other conditions the same.

The aperture likewise affects in-focus ranges, and/or the degree of defocus within a picture.

The following displays the contrast between the degree of aperture and defocus. As can be seen, the background and foreground get more defocused as the f-numbers become smaller.

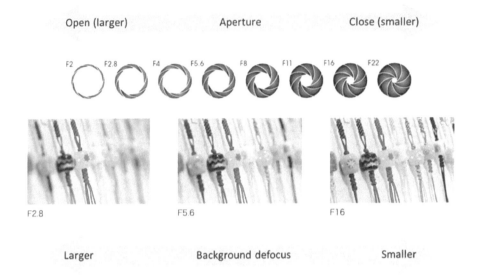

Generally, with smaller f-numbers, more light enters into your camera, which increases the defocus effect. Every lens has its minimal f-number, which is known as the **maximum apertures** of a lens. To find out the maximum apertures of a lens, check the specification of that lens and/or the value displayed on that lens, as displayed in the image below.

Lenses with small f-numbers are generally known as **fast lens**.

Aperture Priority modes (A-mode)

This mode lets you set f-numbers to your taste. Here, your camera automatically selects the ISO sensitivity and shutter speed to shoot well-exposed photographs.

This mode comes in handy when you'd rather defocus the background and foreground, only focusing on your main subject, or whenever you'd rather have a clear rendition of the whole landscape by focusing on wide ranges from the foregrounds to the backgrounds.

Shot with F1.4 to defocus the background

Shot with F11 to shoot the entire image clearly, including the background

As f-numbers become bigger, the opening that allows light into your camera becomes smaller. Due to this, shutter speed slows down, which might cause images to blur due to camera shake.

Creative Look

Creative Look gives you more use of your camera by capturing movies or photos with images processing applied to generate your preferred atmosphere or mood. This feature gives you more room to explore your creativity.

About Creative Look

With images (movies or photos), "look" refers to how they appear or their impression on you, as passed across by numerous details like brightness, sharpness, and color tone.

When you change how you combine the brightness, sharpness, contrast, saturation, color tone, as well as other picture elements, one subject can be given different looks. To bring your vision to life, you could configure images processing with these elements ideally balanced.

There are 10 distinct preset looks on Creative Look. When you choose modes like **VV** or **FL** to bring your visions to life or create looks suitable to the scene, you get more liberty to express yourself. You can likewise personalize preset modes on these advanced images processing to generate more personal looks.

You can use Creative Look for both movies and photos, which makes it ideal for individuals who would like to maintain consistent looks when whenever they are posting across social media right after shooting.

Creative Looks Styles

Creative Looks features and styles are as below. Examples from 4 modes are explained below. While shooting, look at the Live Views display on your camera screen or the viewfinder to select suitable modes for your preferred moods, scenes, or subjects.

FL IN SH

FL

This look enhances the contrast, greenery, and sky while toning down certain colors. This is ideal for capturing natural landscapes showcasing the mountains, sky, sea, or any other subject against the blue sky.

IN

Reduces saturation and contrast, for matte looks. Ideal for creating stately images or elegant atmospheres.

SH

Produces bright atmospheres with vibrancy, softness, and transparency. Ideal for creating soft, gentle moods.

VV2

Produces extremely clear pictures with bright, vivid colors. Causes colourful scenes and subjects to appear more impressive, and likewise enhances dull or pale colors in cloudy weathers or "high-key shooting."

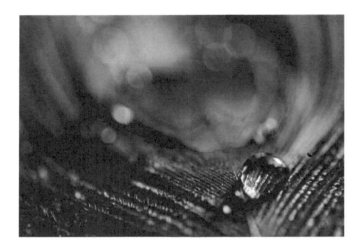

To experience monotone photography, select **SE** modes for sepia tones or **BW** modes for black-and-white pictures.

To Customize Creative Looks

Depending on your chosen mode, clarity, sharpness range, sharpness, saturation, fading, shadows, highlights and contrast can be fine-tuned. After creating your desired look, you could have it saved as custom looks and later applied when needed. Custom Looks likewise allows you to store slightly varying versions of one mode, such that various versions of a favorite mode can be used for various scenes.

How it differs from Picture Profiles

With the Picture Profiles menu, parameters that affect colors, gradation (dark and light tones), as well as other image attributes can be adjusted or changed. Mainly used during movie recordings, this menu comprises advanced settings for modifying detail, color, gamma curve and a spread of different parameters.

This is ideal for individuals involved in video or movie production whose job is to prepare final images by effecting subtle alterations while grading the images using a computer right after shooting.

On cameras featuring Picture Profiles, by default numerous presets are obtainable, S-Log inclusive.

Picture Profiles or Creative Look can both be used in adjusting image textures and colors. You can summarize the difference as follow.

Creative Look

- Easy to setup for both still images and movies.
- Enjoy perceptive image processing even though you lack special knowledge. This is ideal for beginners.

Picture Profile

- Majorly used during movie recordings, but is likewise available for still-images.
- Needs knowledge of color modes, gamma curves, as well as different parameters. After you use this feature in shooting, you will need final editing like grading.
  Enables close matches with the feel and look of pictures from professional videos cameras fitted with S-Log and creates feelings like that of movies on a film.

White Balance

White balance refers to that feature that causes white objects to appear white in photographs, by making up for the influences of the colors of light within a shooting environment.

Various lights have varying characteristics and colors. For instance, an incandescent light has yellowish colors whereas sunlight on cloudy days have bluish casts. For humans, our eyes automatically make up for these influences, based on the idea that "white objects should appear white." Nevertheless, in photographs, cameras reproduce captured colors as they are. Due to this, based on ambient light, white might appear bluish or yellowish in photographs, as against the actual picture as viewed by the human eye.

In picture [1], white dishes appear yellowish due to the incandescent lights whereas picture [2] has bluish casts due to the sunlight.

The original function of white balance is to alter the degree of **whiteness** in your camera, to correct for **colors casting** such as this resulting from the colors of light. Alongside this function of replicating whiteness, in a digital camera, white balance functions are increasingly used in the capacity of color filters to also alter color tones.

[1]   [2]

Auto white-balance (AWB)

Your camera has **auto white-balance (AWB)** functions, which automatically alters white balance in accordance with detected scenes. Since, by default, the white-balance functions of cameras are set at AWB, it automatically alters the colors of pictures to appear natural in different scenes. In scenarios with mixed lightings or for snapshots, whenever you're unable to decide the suitable white-balance setting, it is advised that you begin with AWB.

To change white balance settings

Alongside AWB, various white-balance settings ideal for different scenes are preset within your camera. If you're experiencing difficulty getting your expected colors with AWB, and/or you'd rather alter color tones in accordance with your tastes, you could manually choose the preferred white balance settings.

AWB (Auto WB)	☀-1 (Fluor.: Warm White)
☀ (Daylight)	☀0 (Fluor.: Cool White)
☁ (Shade)	☀+1 (Fluor.: Day White)
☁ (Cloudy)	☀+2 (Fluor.: Daylight)
☼ (Incandescent)	WB (Flash)

As displayed in the above figure, 10 white-balance settings, AWB included, are preset within your camera. The below pictures displays color differences using various white-balance settings.

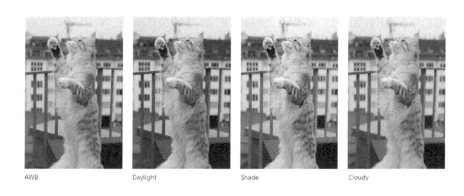

AWB   Daylight   Shade   Cloudy

The kitten was shot when it was cloudy. With **Cloudy** and **AWB**, colors were naturally reproduced, similar to the real colors. In contrast, the picture has more bluish cast under **Daylight**, as well as a more yellowish cast with **Shade**.

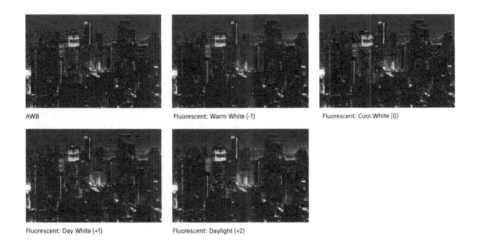

AWB

Fluorescent: Warm White (-1)

Fluorescent: Cool White (0)

Fluorescent: Day White (+1)

Fluorescent: Daylight (+2)

Now, we will contrast the night views shots above. In this scenario, **AWB** replicates the real colors very well though the entire picture has some green casts. When you change to **Fluorescent**, the whole green cast disappears. Amongst the settings under **Fluorescent**, you'll see the colors grow warmer as the settings change from – to +. Choose settings on the basis of your preference or the picture you'll like to capture.

Fine-Tuning

You can fine-tune every white-balance setting. When you fine-tune preset white-balance settings, you can apply personal touches to your picture.

- White-balance settings that you can fine-tune as well as their operation screen varies by model.

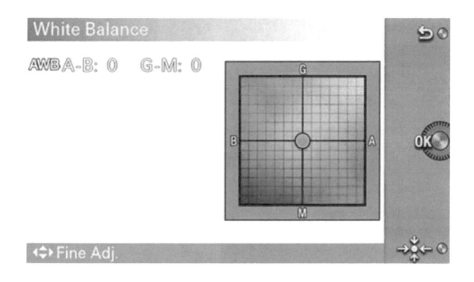

The picture at the right was captured by adding blue tinges to **AWB** settings.

Fine-tuning options makes it possible for you to render colors that can't be gotten via the preset white-balance settings.

White balance: AWB

After fine-tuning

Utilizing white-balance for photographic expressions

White balance function was originally created to alter **whiteness**. However, this adjustment isn't always the final answer. You might like your picture to be cooler or warmer depending on your desired theme or personal preferences. You can use white balance for this type of expressions. Let us consider different color renderings by combining various colors with white-balance.

S-Mode and Shutter Speed

Shutter speed refers to the duration for which shutters at the front of image sensors are open. During the time the shutter stays open, it exposes the image sensors to light, which helps with the creation of images.

[1] The shutter is open.   [2] The shutter is closed.

The above images display the shutter portion of E-mount cameras. In [1], you have the shutter open with the image sensors exposed to lights. The amount of light that gets into the image sensors increases with the length of the shutter speeds. For instance, if you change the shutter speed from 1/60sec to 1/30sec, it doubles the quantity of light.

Alongside aperture which alters the quantity of light entering the lens, shutter speed, alongside other factors determine exposure. In **A**-modes, **P**-modes, and automatic shooting modes, your camera automatically determines its shutter speed. Under **S**-mode, shutter speed can be set to your taste.

Effects of shutter speeds on photographs

You can regulate photographic expressions by changing shutter speeds. The following pictures display how they appear based on shutter speed.

[1] 1/1250 sec   [2] 1/20 sec   [3] 1/4 sec

These images of waterfalls were captured while changing shutter speeds.

Picture [1] was captured at 1/1250sec and is the fastest shutter speed of all three. Since the shutters were opened briefly, it captured moments where it appears that the water has stopped its motion. Picture [2] was captured at 1/20sec. Since the water was flowing while the shutters were open, the picture appears more dynamic. Picture [3] was captured at 1/4sec, which is the slowest speed. Leaving the shutter open for extended periods resulted in silky renderings of water flows.

With this, you can experience different renderings of moving subjects by altering shutter speed. Shutter speed can be set to your taste under **M**-mode and **S**-mode, however the ranges of available speed differs by models.

To take shots freezing the motion of moving subjects, like when capturing sports scenes, it is recommended that you use the fastest obtainable shutter speeds, such that you prevent image blur resulting from the subject's fast motion.

Shutter speed: 1/4000 sec

By taking shots at 1/4000sec, the above picture captured the instant when the subject tried to get the ball. Conversely, when you'd rather capture a light trail or flow of water, it is recommended that you use slower shutter speeds.

Shutter speed: 5 sec

When you set shutter speeds to 5sec, the above picture captures the trail of fireworks. Nevertheless, the slower a shutter speed becomes, the easier it becomes for images to get blurred. When you shoot in low-light scenarios like night views and fireworks, where shutter speeds tend to automatically slow down, it is crucial that you use tripods to steady your camera.

In scenes where you're unable to use tripods, you could make use of higher shutter speeds when you increase ISO sensitivity. Nevertheless, bear in mind that higher ISO sensitivities tend to result in noise on your images. Also, to capture a night view while holding your camera with your hands, it is best that you opt for the **Hand-held Twilights** mode under Scenes Selections.

Shutter speed: 0.5 sec

Because the picture above was captured with slow shutter speeds, the images blur due to camera shake. When you capture moving subjects, apply caution so as not to blur the images, which could result from the motion of the subject, alongside camera shake. When either the camera or the subject is in motion, the picture becomes blurred and the outcome is an unclear picture.

Shutter Priority modes (S-mode)

This mode allows you set shutter speed however you like. Here, your camera automatically selects the ISO sensitivity and aperture (f-number) to capture well-exposed pictures.

This mode comes in handy for capturing shots that freeze the motions of moving subjects, or capture light or water trails.

ISO Sensitivity

In a digital camera, ISO sensitivity indicates the extent to which light from your lens gets amplified within the camera. The quantity of light entering your camera is influenced by your shutter speed and aperture. From this quantity, light gets amplified to generate well-exposed images. ISO sensitivity denotes the numerical level of the amplification.

For instance, ISO200 is double the sensitivity of ISO100. This implies that when you alter the settings to ISO200, it allows you shoot images with the exact brightness of ISO100 even under half of the quantity of light.

Actually, with majority of modes, the camera automatically determines ISO sensitivity in accordance with shooting conditions. Nevertheless, with **P/A/S/M**-modes, ISO sensitivity can be manually set based on your preferences.

With increase in sensitivity, a faster shutter speed can be used even under low-light environments to minimize blurs resulting from camera shake in low lighting or the movement of subjects when shooting sports scenes. However, since the light gets amplified electrically, capturing with high ISO sensitivities tends to cause loss in sharpness or more grain (noise) in the photograph.

[1] ISO: 3200   [2] ISO: 800

The night view pictures above were captured with handheld camera, with ISO3200 and ISO800 for [1] and [2] respectively. When you adjust the settings to high sensitivities, it prevents image blur, though the building in the left photograph appears grainy.

Differences between Manual focus (MF) and Autofocus (AF) Modes

Autofocus (AF) refers to the camera's ability to automatically focus on subjects. Majority of digital cameras have this feature enabled. There are different AF methods; the available ones are dependent on the model of the camera. You can use different modes in accordance with your subject or scene.

Autofocus methods

This section discusses AF techniques of α-series.

The two major AF methods are AF-C and AF-S, and both of them have varying focus operations right after you partly push the shutter tab down.

- **Single-shot AF (AF-S):** Autofocus functions when you partly push the shutter tab down. Once your subject comes into focus, focus gets locked. It is ideal for capturing motionless subjects like snapshots or landscapes.
- **Continuous AF (AF-C):** Autofocus keeps functioning and adjusting focus while you partly push and hold the shutter tab down. It is ideal for capturing subjects like railway or sports photography.
- **AF-A (Automatic AF):** When you partly push the shutter tab down, your camera automatically detects if your subjects are in motion or not, and switches AF modes between AF-C and AF-S accordingly. This mode should be used to capture different subjects simultaneously, or to prevent the manual switching of AF modes.

Direct manuals focus (DMF)

You can manually carry out fine adjustments right after executing auto focusing, allowing you to focus on subjects more quickly compared to when you use manual focus right from the start. This is handy is situations like macro shooting.

Manual focus (MF)

This function allows photographers to adjust focus manually in place of their camera. Though autofocus shooting is more common with digital cameras, Manual focus comes in handy when it is difficult to focus with autofocus, like during macro shooting. In manual focus, you can alter focus positions by rotating your lens' focus ring. Check the Handbook or Instruction Manual on your camera to find out how to change to Manual focus modes and/or detailed operations.

Above is a picture of SEL24105G lens; the focus ring is part **A**. Whenever you set your camera to MF modes, you can manually adjust its focus by rotating its focus ring.

Lens: SAL50M28 / Focal length: 50 mm / F-number: 4.0

The picture above was captured with macro lenses SAL50M28. It is focusing on the drop of water towards the left front part, whereas the background and foreground are extremely defocused. Whenever you need to precisely adjust its focus to small regions as seen in this instance, it is recommended that you use MF. MF likewise comes in handy whenever your camera is unable to locate your preferred focus positions via autofocus.

MF Assist and Focus Magnifier

When using manual focus to shoot, you can use MF Assist and Focus Magnifier functions to confirm if your subject is under focus. How available these functions are as well as their detailed functionalities differ in accordance with the model of your camera. Certain models only have one of these functionalities, though you can use that function to enlarge parts of your subjects that you'll like to focus on, to manually fine-tune the focus.

Check the Handbook and User Manual for your particular model to know more about the functions available on it as well as info about settings.

[Focus Magnifier] display on the α55. The area in the orange frame is magnified.

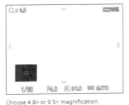

Choose 4.8× or 9.5× magnification.

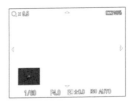

When you assign both MF Assist and Focus Magnifier to customizable keys or buttons, you can set focus magnifications time to [Infinite], which comes in handy for pictures of a starry sky or macro photography using tripods.

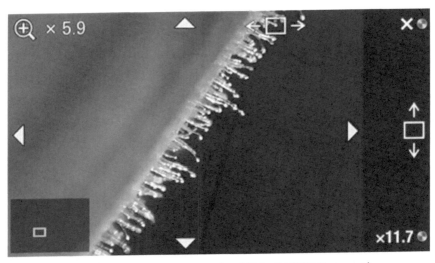

Macro photography focus adjustment using MF Assist (NEX-7 camera)

Peaking

This function improves the outline of in-focus areas while shooting with Direct Manuals Focus or Manual Focus. With Peaking, it is much easier to detect in-focus areas by outlining them in color. You can select a display color.

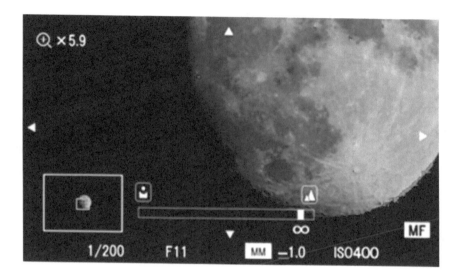

Drive Mode

With drive mode, you can choose shooting options like **Self-timer** or **Continuous Shooting**. The obtainable modes differ in accordance with your camera model. This section discusses general drive modes popular for majority of cameras.

Single Shooting

This ☐ is its regular shooting mode. It shoots one image with the touch of the shutter tab. (If you perform composite shooting in modes like Superior Auto, it might release the shutter several times for one picture.)

Continuous Shooting

Images are continuously ▦ shot while you press and hold the shutter tab down. Based on your model, you could likewise choose the continuous shooting speed.

Self-timer

A shot is taken with self-timer ↻ 2 or 10 seconds after pressing the shutter tab. The ten-second timer is handy for letting the photographer join the picture whereas the two-second self-timer helps in minimizing camera shake during shoots, like when capturing night views with tripods.

Remote Commander

This mode 📶 helps you capture images using Wireless Remotes Commander (not sold together).

Manual Exposure (M mode)

In manual exposure (**M** mode), the photographer has the ability to alter sensitivity, shutter speed, and aperture. In **S**, **A**, and **P** modes, your camera determines image brightness (optimal exposure), but with **M** mode, the settings of the user determine exposure. This mode is handy for instances where you'd like to both control the shutter speed and aperture or whenever you'd like to capture starry skies, fireworks as well as other unique subjects.

Based on their models, certain cameras allow the automatic setting of sensitivity even under **M** mode. Whenever you set sensitivity to auto, sensitivity automatically changes to offer adequate exposure in accordance with the set shutter speed and aperture. Additionally, you can also use exposure compensation.

One of the capture modes

Focal length: 16 mm (35 mm equivalent) / f-stop: 2.8 / Shutter speed: 30 seconds

Bulb Photography

Alongside **M** mode, bulb photography is another feature. Here, the shutter stays open for the length of time in which you push the shutter tab. This is handy for instances where you'd like to open then shutter for thirty seconds or longer, for instance, when capturing the lengths of a firework trail. You can make use of bulb photography when you choose **BULB** under shutter speed. Rotate the dial towards the directions of increase over **30"** to show **BULB**.

When you use your finger to press the shutter tab down, it tends to result in blurring of your shot, so ensure that you use remotes commanders and tripods with bulb mode.

For precautions and detailed settings whenever you use bulb mode, check the Handbook and User Manual of your model.

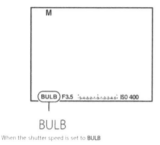

BULB

When the shutter speed is set to **BULB**

Focal length: 28 mm (35 mm equivalent) / f-stop: 14 / Shutter speed: 23 seconds

BEGINNERS TIPS

Shooting spectacular portraits with highlighted people

Whenever you emphasize people and defocus backgrounds, you can capture spectacular pictures with clear themes.

These pictures are referred to as portraits, and you can use this technique for day-to-day snapshots, alongside memorial pictures at wedding or birthday events.

Whenever you are shooting unintentionally, the entire figure of the person is normally included within the frame. This brings about monotonous compositions such as with ID photo. Here you'll learn certain tips for highlighting people and finishing up your pictures more impressively.

When shooting, ensure you set your camera to **A**-mode and leave the aperture open as long as possible.

Shooting with telephoto side

When using zoom lenses, get very close to your subject and capture with the telephoto end (with lengthier focal lengths). This way, you're able to remove undesired surrounding items and increase the defocus of the backgrounds, such that you only emphasize the person.

[1] Focal length: 55 mm /
F-number: 1.8

[2] Focal length: 55 mm /
F-number: 1.8

In the above example, picture [2] was captured by getting very close to your subjects and zooming-in on their upper body. Due to this, expressions of your subjects are emphasized and more expressively rendered. Shooting at close ranges causes backgrounds to be more defocused as well as highlights the woman's expressions.

For memento shoots in tourist locations, pictures such as [1], which adds surrounding landscapes into the frame, might be better. Nevertheless, if you'd rather only emphasize the person, [2] appears more impressive.

Consider its composition

Changing compositions results in significant differences in the atmospheres of pictures, even when you're shooting one particular subject.

With casual shooting, there is the tendency to compose photographs with subjects at the middle of the frames. When shooting portraits, nevertheless, attempt using the "Rule-of-Thirds" for your compositions.

In "Rule-of-Thirds" compositions, it divides the frame into nine sections (3 horizontal by 3 vertical), while it places your main subject at the intersections of dividing lines. When shooting

48

portraits, position the middle of the eyes or face at the intersections.

The "Rule-of-Thirds" is at the root of well-balanced pictures. If you're unsure of how best to compose a shot, attempt using the "Rule-of-Thirds." When you note this rule, you'll be able to automatically capture many good pictures. α-cameras have a feature that shows the gridlines for the "Rule-of-Thirds" on your monitor towards the back of your camera. This function should be used whenever you need guides for your compositions when shooting.

Focal length: 70 mm / F-number: 4.0 / Shutter speed: 1/250 sec.

Just by putting the middle of their head at the dividing lines, the shot above becomes well-balanced and really impressive. Moreover, when you leave space within the region your subject is looking, the picture conveys the air of that moment.

Also, like its basic principle, portrait photographs should be captured with vertical orientations, just like with the picture above.

When you place your subject's body parallel against the longer sides of the picture, it naturally organizes the backgrounds, making it easy for you to make the picture clear and simple. If you'd rather include the backgrounds, then you can shoot with horizontal orientation. However, if you'd rather just emphasize the person, it's definitely recommended that you use vertical orientations.

To use back light

The angle of lighting is another thing to note. Particularly when capturing portrait pictures of women, their hair and skins are rendered softly when you use the back light to shoot. For ideal back light, avoid daytimes when the sun is at its strongest, and take your shots later in the afternoons when sunlight is weaker, or during cloudy days when possible. If it is imperative that you shoot when the sun is at its strongest, try finding ways of weakening the light, like shooting under trees.

Conversely, when you use the front light in shooting, it creates shadows on faces, and the expressions of your subjects would be grim due to the strong lighting. If you're able to regulate the light angle, try creating back light.

When you use the backlight to shoot, however, faces might get dark. When this happens, adjust exposure via the exposure compensations function to increase the brightness of the face. Though it'll whiten the backgrounds a little, it will also promote a soft atmosphere round the subject.

Focal length: 200 mm / F-number: 4.0 / Shutter speed: 1/400 sec.

This is the portrait of a woman captured with back light. The light illuminates the subject from behind towards the left end. There aren't any shadows on the face, and the light on the hair gives off an airy and soft look.

Using fixed focal lengths lenses

It is recommended that you use fixed focal lengths lenses to increase the defocus of your backgrounds and only emphasize the subject. Since fixed focal lengths lenses allow large amounts of light into a camera, they could minimize blurring whenever you shoot in low-light environments, portraits included.

Focal length: 35 mm / F-number: 2 / Shutter speed: 1/400 sec.

SEL35F18F

Providing impressive image qualities even at its highest F1.8 aperture, this lightweight and compact 35mm prime lens designed for full-framed cameras is ideal for all types of pictures ranging from table top pictures to outdoor shoots. Precise, quiet, and fast AF operations as well as trustworthy AF tracking makes it ideal for shooting stills and videos.

Focal length: 50 mm / F-number: 2 / Shutter speed: 1/250 sec.

SEL50F18F

Large-apertures 50mm prime lenses are compulsory for core full-framed cameras users; this is a spectacular and affordable choice. It has state-of-the-art optical designs for high quality images, and its large F1.8 maximal aperture produces beautiful background bokeh. With APS-C formats E-mounts bodies, it equally offers high quality with equivalent focal lengths of around 75mm.

Focal length: 55 mm / F-number: 2.8 / Shutter speed: 1/640 sec.

SEL55F18Z

Standard prime lenses with 55mm focal lengths and maximum apertures of F1.8 provides outstanding ZEISS Sonnar contrasts as well as resolutions for full-framed E-mounts bodies. It is also able to create beautiful backgrounds bokeh to set-off subjects when needed. Its large, bright maximal aperture implies that you can take handheld shots in low-light environments while retaining outstanding clarity and sharpness.

Focal length: 85 mm / F-number: 1.8 / Shutter speed: 1/1600 sec.

SEL85F18

The smooth bokeh and sharpness of this well-executed mid-range telephotos prime lenses makes it ideal for shooting portraits – the SEL85F18 stands out in a class of its own. It comprises compact, lightweight designs for mobility, alongside high-performance optics as well as a large maximum aperture of F1.8 which delivers impressive image quality. This is another must-have lens for individuals that use both APS-C and full-framed cameras.

Give soft touches to shots of flowers

To add a soft touch and gentle feel to shots of flowers, their backgrounds as well as the degree of defocus are crucial. To increase defocus levels, set your camera to A-mode and widen the aperture as far as it can go.

To create background defocus

To shoot the beautiful colors and softness of flowers, how you render the background plays a major role. Using the directions under Defocus Factors, get within distance of your subject, and use the telephoto end of your lens to shoot (with lengthier focal lengths). Through this process, the flowers are highlighted and the degree of defocus is increased, letting you shoot pictures that are a bit different from the norm.

[1] Focal length: 55mm   [2] Focal length: 210mm

The picture above was captured with varying focal lengths: 55mm and 210mm for [1] and [2] respectively. As is evident, shots with longer focal lengths create greater backgrounds defocus and place emphasis on the flower's freshness. If you can get your hands on telephoto lenses, you can use it to more effectively render your backgrounds.

Also, picture [2] takes more creative liberty with its background colors. Since the whole background is made up of green colors that contrast with red, it enhances how vivid your flower appears. attempt shooting from various angles using various backgrounds, till you find your preferred shot.

To adjust the brightness

When you slightly brighten the image, it enhances how soft your flowers appear. In the instance below, picture [1] was captured with the camera automatically adjusting the exposure. Since it has a bright background, the flowers were rendered a bit dark. This picture attempts to pass across the shape and color of those flowers, though the pink appears a bit dull. A bit brightened by exposures compensation, picture [2] has a more gentle and soft atmosphere.

[1] Exposure compensations: 0   [2] Exposure compensations: +1.3

Likewise, when shooting images at home and/or in places where you're able to regulate the light angle, attempt positioning the flowers such that they're illuminated by backlight. Where possible, light entering through your curtain can be used in place of direct sunlight, and/or shoot on cloudy days. These shooting conditions are best for creating soft lighting.

To try macro lenses

When shooting small items or flowers, you might want to get really close to your subjects to get close-ups shots. However, lenses have minimum focusing distances which limit how close you're allowed to get to subjects. In such scenarios, "Macro lenses" are your go-to lenses allowing you get very close to your subjects and capture close-up shots.

F-number: 5.6/Shutter speed: 1/15sec.

SEL90M28G

This is leading E-mounts medium telephotos macro lenses has inbuilt image stabilization and delivers impressive G-Lens quality: Stunning resolutions at a magnification of about 1:1, alongside beautiful backgrounds bokeh when needed, even when images are captured handheld. Its floating focus mechanisms ensure that you achieve constantly superior optical performances at every focusing distance.

Focal length: 50mm/F-number: 2.8/Shutter speed: 1/640sec.

SEL50M28

This is a versatile 50mm "regular" macro prime lenses designed for full-framed sensors and is handy for day-to-day photography alongside shooting stunning 1:1 macro pictures. This allows you get within 6.3" of your subjects while its normal viewing angle allows you add background features for increased creative liberty. Operation and controls are optimized for convenient, effective close-up shootings.

Focal length: 30mm/F-number: 3.5/Shutter speed: 1/500sec.

SEL30M35

The lightweight and compact body of this lens provides widespread, high-performance macro functionalities. It is really a 1:1 macro lens fitted with minimum working distances of 2.4cm that allows for the rendering of tiny details and subjects with excellent contrast and resolution.

Capturing dynamic landscapes

When you encounter extensive landscapes while travelling, it makes sense for you to want a pictorial rendition of its looks, its brisk atmosphere and magnificence included.

To take those types of pictures, set your camera to **A**-mode and use the procedures below.

Use smaller apertures to shoot

First, smaller apertures should be used in shooting landscapes. Set its aperture value to about F8 to bring the whole picture sharply in focus, though recommended values might differ in accordance with the lenses or shooting conditions.

Generally, to shoot sharp pictures with high contrasts, the F-number should be increased. Conversely, to add soft feels to the whole picture, reduce the F-number.

Captured with apertures set at F9.0, this picture appears sharp, focusing on both the pine at the front as well as the sky at the background. With very small F-numbers, the pictures tend to lack crispness, as just either the sky or tree comes into focus.

Focal length: 16mm/F-number: 9.0/Shutter speed: 1/30sec.

Capturing wide ranges on the wide-angled sides

When you use zoom lenses to shoot landscapes, you can shoot the wide ranges of scenes whenever you use your lens' the wide-angled side (with smaller focal lengths). Likewise, whenever you shoot landscapes comprising the sky, occupying larger areas of the picture with the sky gives you a broader impression and conveys the magnificence of that scene.

This picture was captured using the wide-angled sides of a zoom lens. Though the ocean is the major subject, the impressive atmosphere is boosted when you fill larger areas with the clouds and sky, in place of only capturing the ocean in the whole frame.

Focal length: 16mm/F-number: 11/Shutter speed: 1/800sec.

Enhancing vividness and sharpness

In order to render clouds and landscapes more vividly and sharply, change the settings under Creative Look/ creative Style. Choosing the setting for [Landscape] enhances the saturation and contrasts and finishes up the picture with heightened image depth. Adjust "Contrast" and "Saturation" under options settings for increased contrast in shadows or colors for an increasingly impressive finish. You can fine-tune every parameter using ±3 step.

These pictures were captured using varying Creative Look/Creative Style settings. Picture [1] was captured using [Standard]. Picture [2], on the other hand, was captured with [Landscape] with "Contrast" and "Saturation" enhanced under option settings. Due to this, the colored leaves and sky are reproduced powerfully and vividly. However, apply caution so as not to extremely enhance saturation and contrast. This might result in pictures that appear like painted pictures due to color saturation.

Try wide-angled lenses

To capture dynamic images with wide viewing angles, it is recommended that you use wide-angled lenses. Wide-angle lenses capture wider ranges of scenes compared to the human eye. Due to this, you can experience shooting distinct pictures in day-to-day street shots and snapshots, alongside landscape photography.

Focal length: 12mm/F-number: 16/Shutter speed: 1/5sec.

SEL1224G

This compact 12mm to 24mm ultra-wide-angled zoom lens has the shortest available focal lengths in any full-framed E-mounts lens, alongside impressive corner-to-corner G-Lens resolutions at every aperture. It's ideal for architecture photography and dynamic landscapes. Its impressive mobility and precise, fast, quiet autofocus makes it the go-to choice for shooting stills as well as movies.

F-number: 8/Shutter speed: 1/100sec.

SEL1635Z

This full-framed E-mount 16 to 35mm ZEISS Vario-Tessar zoom gives impressive performance in compact, lightweight packages. Its versatile zoom ranges coupled with inbuilt optical images stabilization makes it the ideal choice for landscapes, group shots, indoor scenes, snapshots, and lots more, particularly with full-framed α7-series body. Its constant F4 maximal aperture facilitates depth-of-field control and exposure.

To try fixed focal lengths lenses

Focal length: 35mm/F-number: 8/Shutter speed: 1/400sec.

SEL35F18F

This offers impressive image qualities even at its peak aperture of F1.8; its lightweight and compact 35mm prime lenses for full-framed cameras makes it ideal for all types of pictures ranging from tabletop pictures to outdoor shoots. Its quiet, precise, and fast AF operations as well as its trustworthy AF tracking makes it ideal for shooting stills and videos.

Focal length: 24mm/F-number: 11/Shutter speed: 1/250sec.

SEL24F18Z

This first-class 24mm (35mm full-framed equivalent) prime lenses feature large F1.8 maximal apertures and is able to carry out impressive contrast and sharpness all through the frame alongside its gorgeous "bokeh" in areas that are out of focus. 0.25 is the maximum magnification for dramatic 1:4 close-up capabilities, as well as internal drives motor offers quiet, smooth autofocus operations that are appreciated by moviemakers.

How to capture delicious-looking food pictures

Whenever you are shooting desserts or dishes, you'll want your pictures to give off the deliciousness of your subjects. To shoot these types of pictures, check out brightness and color, such that you're able to trap the appealing look of your food exactly how it appears.

First, set your camera to **P**-mode, and attempt the techniques below.

Reproducing colors exactly how you want

Brightness and color are essential to making pictures of desserts and dishes appear delicious.

First, use white balance to adjust color. White balance allows you regulate standard "white", though it can likewise be used as color filters with digital cameras. Use auto white-balance [AWB] to shoot first to confirm the outcome of the shoot. Afterwards, try [Cloudy] or [Daylight] where necessary. If you're still searching for your preferred color, you can make use of the fine-tuning feature for white-balance.

Generally, dishes appear more appealing when you shoot them with a bit of warm color (reddish tint).

These pictures were captured with varying white-balance settings. Captured using [AWB], picture [1] appears whiter as against the actual picture due to the source of light within the restaurant. Picture [2] was captured using [Daylight]. Using warmer colors added the tantalizing finish to the picture.

[1] White-balance: AWB   [2] White-balance: Daylight

Considering the angle of light

The brightness and lighting angle are likewise important. Dishes appear more appealing when captured using back light. Whenever you use the front light in shooting, the color and shape of the dish are clearly rendered. However, since the light doesn't shine through your subject or create shadows on it, the picture appears flat and lack depths.

Picture [1] was captured using front light. Though the shape of the fruits and bread are clearly rendered, the image appears flat, similarly to ID pictures. Direct flash likewise generates front light thus resulting in similar pictures.

Picture [2] was captured using back light. Under shadows, breads get rendered with depths. Additionally, the beverage and fruits appear more appealing due to the picture passing through them. Just by changing the lighting angle, there will be a significant difference in its finish.

[1] Shot using front light [2] Shot using back light

However, when you use the back light to shoot, subjects might appear darker than usual due to their bright backgrounds. When this happens, you can make use of exposure compensations function. When the dish appears dark, you can brighten it by adjusting the exposure towards the +side. The idea is to alter exposure on the basis of the food's brightness: it makes no difference if the background appears a bit whitish.

In picture [3], the dish appears dark due to the presence of strong light entering the lens.

Picture [4] was generated through the application of exposure compensations to the picture at the left. When you adjust exposure on the basis of the dish to brighten it, it now appears more delicious.

[3] Exposure compensations: 0 [4] Exposure compensations: +1

Changing compositions

If you attempt shooting a whole dish, the outcome is most times an unappealing documentary picture. When you pay increased focus to composition, you'll be able to enhance the picture's atmosphere. In the pictures below, [1] shot the whole meal from the vantage point of the eyes of the photographer. You'll be able to view the contents of that dish, though the picture appears pointless and flat. Additionally, with the silverware and dishes within the frame, the pictures have a cluttered appearance.

To enhance this, [2] was captured by getting very close to the food. The dish was captured very closely such that it was a bit outside the frame. The picture has more feel of a presence and communicates how appealing the meal is best. Its background is likewise very organized. Also, it is recommended that you shoot using the diagonal (with your camera tilted) or vertical orientation due to how effective they are at conveying depth.

1   2

To try fixed focal lengths lenses

Fixed focal lengths lenses are handy for food photography, since they are able to generate impressive background defocus. Additionally, since fixed focal lengths lenses allow large amounts of light into your camera, they're likewise ideal for performing indoor shoots in dim lighting.

Focal length: 35mm/F-number: 1.8/Shutter speed: 1/80sec.

SEL35F18F

Offers impressive picture quality even at maximal F1.8 apertures, this lightweight and impressive 35mm prime lenses for full-framed cameras are the go-to choice for all types of photography ranging from table top photography to outdoor shoots. Quiet, precise, fast AF operations as well as reliable AF trackings makes it ideal for shooting stills and videos.

Focal length: 50mm/F-number: 1.8/Shutter speed: 1/100sec.

SEL50F18F

Large apertures 50mm prime lenses are essential for professional full-framed camera users, making this an affordable, excellent choice. For high picture quality, it has state-of-the-art optical designs, and its large F1.8 maximal aperture produces beautiful backgrounds bokeh. On APS-C formats E-mounts bodies, it offers equal high qualities with equivalent focal lengths of approximately 75mm.

Capturing cute expressions on your pets

Whenever you take snapshots of your pets, trusting relationships with them is the key. Simply pointing your camera at them might cause them to become extremely cautious. So, allow your pets to first get accustomed to a camera bit by bit in relaxed environments, like your home.

Let's begin by using **P**-mode to capture using the settings selected automatically by your camera.

Focal length: 120mm/F-number: 4.0/Shutter speed: 1/100sec

Capture relaxed images of the pets in your home, exactly as you see them. Alongside taking live shots of the pets, try capturing numerous shots and expressions.

Shooting from the eye level of your pets

First, squat and capture images from the eye level of your pets. When you shoot from your eye level as a human, which we normally do, your camera is facing downwards. Due to this, the background comprises just the floor or ground, and it is quite difficult to get defocus effects. When you shoot from the level of your pets, you can take snapshots as viewed from the eyes of your pets and save your preferred pretty expressions from different angles and directions.

To capture images from the level of your pets, make use of the monitor's tilt feature towards the back of your camera.

You can simply view a scene from the eye level of your pets when you look downwards into your monitor from the top. The obtainable tilt angles as well as monitor shape might differ by camera models.

The best picture opportunities don't only come whenever your pets are directly looking into the camera; they also come whenever your pets are excited about toys or food. This allows you shoot interesting scenes, different from the norm. Try taking pictures of your friends or family having a fun time with the pets.

Focal length: 120mm/F-number: 4.0/Shutter speed: 1/160sec

This picture captured the expressions of the cat looking at its food above. When you shoot from low levels, almost from the floor, it creates a different atmosphere from ordinary shots taken from front. Additionally, when you move some distance from your subject and use the telephoto end (with lengthier focal lengths) of your zoom lens to shoot, it increases the defocus of the background, emphasizing the expression of the cat. Conversely, when you get quite close and capture images using the wide-angled side (with short focal lengths), the entire body of your pet will occupy the frame, causing the picture to appear more powerful and dynamic.

Applying caution to minimize subject blur

Whenever your pets are in motion, blur might occur due to their movement (subject blur). **S**-mode should be used whenever this happens.

By choosing a fast shutter speed under **S**-mode, subject blur is reduced. Although the recommended shutter speed differs in accordance with the movement of your pet and the environment, you'll generally rather take pictures using 1/250sec or faster.

Since it has a slow shutter speed, the picture was unclear and blurred.

The quantity of light filtering into your camera is quite small in dull indoor scenarios. Due to this, when you extremely increase shutter speed, the picture might become dark. When this occurs, the best way around it is to increase the brightness of that room. If you're unable to adjust the room's brightness, or you'd rather shoot under dim lighting, attempt taking repeated shots while slowly reducing shutter speed till the picture appears sufficiently bright. Also, having rapid fixed focal lengths lenses are handy for these types of scenes.

Shutter speed: 1/13sec

To try fixed focal lengths lenses

When using a small F-number (rapid maximum aperture), fixed focal lengths lenses can generate significant backgrounds defocus. Additionally, since they permit large amounts of light into your camera, you'll enjoy taking shots with minimal chances of blurring even in dim lighting indoors.

Focal length: 35mm/F-number: 1.8/Shutter speed: 1/640sec.

SEL35F18F

Offers impressive image qualities even at maximum F1.8 apertures, this lightweight and compact 35mm prime lenses for full-framed cameras is an ideal choice for all types of pictures ranging from table top pictures to outdoor shoots. Quiet, precise, fast AF operations as well as trustworthy AF tracking makes it ideal for shooting stills and videos.

Focal length: 50mm/F-number: 4.0/Shutter speed: 1/80sec

SEL50F18

This midrange telephotos lens with a focal length of 50mm is ideal for portraiture. Its circular aperture and large aperture designs can create gorgeously defocused backgrounds. Also, when used alongside the inbuilt Optical SteadyShots image stabilization systems, it can capture clear and crisp pictures under low-light environments.

Shoot skyscapes

The sky displays different faces each day. Here, you'll learn how to apply finishing to your sky image to create works of art based off your own images. First, set your camera to **P**-mode, and afterwards use the following steps to get your desired picture.

Adjusting color to replicate it to your taste

First, alter color in accordance with your taste using white-balance. The weather and time of the shoot influences the outcome of white-balance. Use every one of the settings to discover your preferred   color.

Below are pictures of the morning sky captured using three varying white-balance settings.

[Daylight]   [Shade]   [Incandescent]

While the picture with the closest resemblance to the real image was captured using [Daylight], choosing [Shade] setting improves the sunlight's warmth. Conversely, when you choose [Incandescent] setting, it adds strong blue casts and creates fantasy-like atmospheres.

Improving image depth

Alongside color adjustment, brightness and contrast can likewise make significant difference in the picture's atmosphere. You can adjust contrast using Creative Look/Creative Style. For instance, if you'll like to emphasize the instability and depth of the sky through the clear rendering of the clouds, as seen in picture [1] below, it is recommended that you use Landscape. This setting emphasizes depth and contrast in the picture. Conversely, if you'll like to render the winter sky using a tranquil appearance, as seen in picture [2], choose [Standard] settings and reduce the values for "Contrast" and "Saturation" under option settings.

[1] [Landscape] [2]   [Standard] Saturation: -2

Last but not least, attempt altering the brightness. You can use exposure compensation to adjust the brightness.

In the scenario below, exposure was altered towards the -side for a clearer rendering of the color and also improve the contrast. Since the ideal levels of exposure compensations vary in accordance with your preference as well as the condition of the sky, capture several images using varying levels.

Exposure compensations: 0   Exposure compensations: -1

Adjusting exposure towards the -side deepens the sky's color and finishes up the picture with improved depth. Conversely, adjusting towards the +side is effective for getting softer finishes with lower contrasts.

Use these three functions – exposure, Creative Look/Creative Style, and white balance – to finish your works to your taste.

Trying a circular polarizing filter

Whenever you use circular polarizing filters, reflected lights within the air can be screened-out, such that the green leaves and blue sky can be more vividly rendered. It likewise suppresses reflections bounding off the surfaces of glass or water.

Without filter   With filter

VF-xxCPAM2

Circular polarizing filters that suppress undesired reflections off water and glass, giving your pictures increased professional looks. It likewise comprises Carl Zeiss T* coatings to minimize ghosts and flares.

Capture a dramatic night view

Night views of scenic spots or while travelling are extremely popular subjects of photography. Here you'll learn to capture night views beautifully, accurately replicating your impressions of the real scene.

First, set your camera to **P**-mode, and use the tips below.

Shooting with tripods

Tripods are very effective tools for capturing beautiful pictures of night scenes. Whenever you are capturing in low-light environments like a night view, shutter speed becomes slow to increase the quantity of light getting into your camera, also increasing ISO sensitivity. Due to this, the picture might be grainy with increased noise or become unclear due to camera shake.

This picture was captured using shutter speed set at 3.2sec. With this speed, the picture becomes entirely blurred, irrespective of the efforts of the photographer to stay still.

Shutter speed: 3.2sec

If you use a tripod to hold the camera in place, you'll be able to capture clear pictures without blurs even with a slow shutter speed. Simultaneously, set ISO sensitivity at the least possible value. Though this will cause shutter speed to slow down further, blur would no longer be a concern since you secured the camera on the tripod.

Additionally, low ISO sensitivities can minimize noise. Minimal ISO sensitivity values differ by models, but values within the ranges of ISO100 and ISO400 are recommended. Whenever you use tripods, deactivate SteadyShot functions to prevent a malfunction. Additionally, vibrations from your camera due to pressing the shutter tab might result in blur. One way to tackle this is to set the two-second self-timer.

Focal length: 50mm/F-number: 10/Shutter speed: 5 sec/ISO: 200/White balance: Daylight

Shot with tripod, the picture above isn't altered by blur. With the lengthy exposure time, light reflecting off the water appears beautiful, evenly spreading across its surface.

What should be done when there isn't any tripod? if there isn't any tripod, lean on nearby poles or walls, or place your camera on handrails or any other flat surfaces to keep it steady and minimize blur.

If these suggestions don't work, you can use rapid shutter speeds to minimize camera shake. If images blur at shutter speeds automatically selected by your camera, you can increase ISO sensitivity manually. Available maximum values of ISO sensitivities vary by models. As ISO sensitivity increases to ISO6400, ISO12800, and higher, shutter speed becomes higher, causing the picture to be less impacted by blur. Nevertheless, the image might suffer from loss of details and noise.

Focal length: 24mm/F-number: 2.8/Shutter speed: 1/40sec/ISO 3200/White balance: AWB

This picture was captured using ISO3200. Using faster shutter speeds successfully prevents blur. Nevertheless, on examining enlarged images, you'll notice that it is a bit grainy and has noise, as against images captured using lower ISO sensitivities. Likewise, as regards the resolutions of details as well as the texture of water surfaces, pictures captured with tripods appear better compared to this.

When noise is obvious, as seen in this instance, make use of "Hand-held Twilights" mode under Scenes Selections (shooting mode). Here, six pictures are continuously shot by pressing the shutter tab once, and these pictures are merged with high precisions while processing the noise. With this process, you can capture night views with minimal noise, as against normal single shots. However, since "Hand-held Twilights" mode under Scenes Selections is an automatic shooting mode, you'll be unable to change the brightness and color discussed in the following section.

Adjusting the color and brightness

If you've learned to capture images without blur, alter the color and brightness based on that image.

You can adjust the brightness using exposure compensations. Human eyes detect night skies as "dark", whereas it detects illuminations and lights from buildings as "bright". Nevertheless, the camera attempts to render every scene with similar brightness standards, whether bright or dark. Due to this, when capturing night views where there is a mixture of bright parts (such as building lights) or dark parts (such as night skies), exposures determined by your camera might not properly replicate the brightness seen with the human eyes.

With this, it is more difficult to attain your desired outcome when capturing night views; night skies might appear washed out, an/or the color of street illuminations might appear clipped.

Additionally, the picture's brightness is likewise influenced by your camera's settings, like Creative Look/Creative Style settings. First, attempt shooting without exposures compensations, and alter exposure on the basis of the outcome.

Focal length: 120mm/F-number: 6.3/White-balance: Fluorescent: Warm White (-1) Saturation: +3/Exposure compensation: 0 Focal length: 120mm/F-number: 6.3/White balance: Fluorescent: Warm White (-1) Saturation: +3/Exposure compensation: +0.7

Without exposure compensations, this picture became underexposed due to the intensity of the street lights.

It blacked out the cityscape at the back of the building. When you set this exposure to +0.7, it renders the picture with the suitable brightness.

Now, moving on to colors adjustment. White balance can be used in adjusting the general color tone. AWB (auto white-balance), where color tone is automatically determined by the camera, faithfully reproduces the real colors. Nevertheless, when capturing night views of cities, choosing [Fluorescent: Warm White] adds bluish tones. This might be more appropriate for communicating the attributes of artificial lights.

Likewise, strong lights, like illuminations and urban buildings, tend to appear whitish in pictures, and their colors fail to appear as vibrant as expected. When this happens, alter saturation towards the + end via the options settings under Creative Look/Creative Style, such that lights become more colourful and vivid.

Focal length: 16mm/F-number: 6.3/Shutter speed: 13 sec/ISO: 200/White balance: AWB Focal length: 16mm/F-number: 6.3/Shutter speed: 13sec/ISO: 200/White balance: Fluorescent: Warm White(-1) Saturation+3

When you make these types of adjustments, you can capture pictures of night views capturing the dramatic impressions you got from the real scene.

Like the other scenes, ideal color tones for shooting night scenes differs based on your intention and preferences. Fully explore the adjustments functions, such as Creative Look/Creative Style, white balance, and exposure compensation, and discover your preferred shot.

Easy fixed focal lengths lenses

With smaller F-numbers (faster maximum aperture), fixed focal lengths lenses allow large amounts of light into the camera. Due to this, you can capture night views with minimal noise and blurring, even under low-light environments. Additionally, you can capture snapshots or portraits with backgrounds immensely defocused.

Focal length: 24mm/F-number: 2.8/Shutter speed: 0.25sec.

SEL24F18Z

This first-class 24mm (35mm full-frames equivalent) prime lenses feature large F1.8 maximal apertures, capable of impressive contrast and sharpness all through the frame alongside outstanding "bokeh" in areas that are out of focus. 0.25x is the maximum magnification for dramatic 1:4 closeups capabilities, and internal drives motors offer quiet, smooth autofocus operations appreciated by moviemakers.

Focal length: 35mm/F-number: 1.8/Shutter speed: 1/80sec.

SEL35F18F

Offers impressive images quality even at maximum F1.8 apertures; this lightweight and compact 35mm prime lenses for full-framed cameras are an ideal choice for different types of pictures ranging from table top pictures to outdoor shoots. Quiet, precise, fast AF operations and trustworthy AF tracking makes it ideal for shooting stills and videos.

Focal length: 55mm/F-number: 2/Shutter speed: 1/80sec.

SEL55F18Z

Standard prime lenses with focal lengths of 55mm and large maximum apertures of F1.8 offers outstanding ZEISS Sonnar resolution and contrast for full-framed E-mounts bodies. Also, it creates gorgeous backgrounds bokeh to set your subjects off when the need arises. The bright, big, maximum aperture implies that handheld shots can be taken in low-light environments while still giving off outstanding clarity and sharpness.

Capture micro worlds

The most suitable way to enlarge small items and experience the outlook of micro worlds is when you make use of macro lenses specifically designed for this reason. This chapter discusses how to capture images using macro lenses, and it likewise comprises certain techniques for those users without macro lenses. Set your camera to A-mode such that you can alter the defocus level.

Basic rule: Get closer and capture images using the telephoto end

You can shoot magnified subjects with zoom lenses, though this doesn't come any close to images captured with macro lenses. To capture closeups of subjects as well as defocus other regions, note the 2 key rules: "Get very close to your subjects" and "Capture using the telephoto end (with lengthier focal lengths) of your lenses".

This rule also comes in handy for "1. Capture Outstanding Portraits Highlighting the People", "2. Give Soft Touches to Shots of Flowers", etc. Nevertheless, lenses have minimum focusing distances, which limit how close you're allowed to get to subjects, and when you move beyond the specified distance, subjects go out-of-focus. Lenses with extremely brief minimum focusing distances, letting you get very close to subjects, are known as "macro lenses." This chapter discusses shooting procedures with macro lenses.

Lens: SEL1855/Focal length: 55mm/F-number: 5.6/Shutter speed: 1/100sec

This picture was captured at 55mm of your zoom lens "SEL1855" supplied alongside NEX-F3 zoom lenses kit. With normal zoom lenses, this is the largest levels of magnifications possible. Whenever you use macro lenses to shoot, conversely, you can enlarge portions of subjects, as seen in the picture below.

Lens: SEL30M35/Focal length: 30mm/F-number: 3.5/Shutter
speed: 1/160sec

This closeup of the stamens and pistil of the flower was captured using E-mounts macro lenses "SEL30M35." Being able to capture such pictures is a crucial feature of macro lenses.

You can likewise capture closeups of parts of your subjects using zoom lenses with high magnification ratios, though they're incomparable to macro lenses. The picture below was captured at 200mm, the telephoto side of E-mounts zoom lenses "SEL18200," after moving as close as allowed to subjects. High-magnification zoom lenses allow you to experience different photographic expressions, not restricted to capturing far subjects but also shooting subjects' closeups at close ranges, such as macro lenses, as seen in the picture below. This type of lens is ideal for individuals who'll like to try out macro shooting but are undecided about committing to dedicated lenses.

Lens: SEL18200/Focal length: 200mm/F-number: 6.3/Shutter
speed: 1/640sec

Shooting with macro lenses

For capturing magnified images of small items or "macro shooting",
it is best that you use macro lenses designed for this purpose. Macro
lenses have extremely short minimal focusing distances allowing
you get extremely close to your subjects. SAL30M28 for A-mounts
and SEL30M35 for E-mounts are the most ideal first time macro
lenses.

Shot with macro lenses SAL30M28 Focal length: 30mm/F-number:
2.8 Shot with macro lenses SAL50M28 Focal length: 50mm/F-
number: 4.0

Macro lenses fill the whole frame with your subject, capturing interesting pictures that can't be generated with another lens. Additionally, macro lenses have larger F-numbers compared to the remaining fixed focal lengths lenses. When you get quite close to your subject as permitted, however, they create great backgrounds defocus, as against to those from fixed focal lengths lenses with smaller F-numbers. The degree of defocus increases the closer you get to your subject. Due to this, you can capture pictures where both the backgrounds and foregrounds are defocused, as seen in the pictures above.

Here is a closeup of small jewelries with the backgrounds defocused. Since macros lenses give you more flexibility in altering shooting compositions and angles, they are ideal foe capturing small items.

When the whole frame is filled with your subject using macro lenses, focusing on your desired point might be problematic. When this occurs, manually focus on your desired point using MF (manual focus) mode. How you switch to MF mode varies based on the model of your camera. Apply caution after you focus. Since your subjects are enlarged with large defocus levels, even slight movements of the body could significantly alter focus position. Where possible, it's advised that you use tripods to hold your camera in place, to enable you focus on that desired point.

Lens: SEL30M35/Focal length: 30mm/F-number: 3.5/Shutter speed: 1/100sec

Recommended macro lenses for beginners

The first time you use macro lenses, it is recommended that you use "SEL30M35" for E-mounts. They offer outstanding performance and convenient viewing angles at that cost.

Focal length: 90mm/F-number: 13/Shutter speed: 1/125sec.

SEL90M28G

The first E-mounts medium telephotos macro lenses with inbuilt images stabilization offers impressive G-Lens quality: Stunning resolutions at about 1:1 magnification, alongside beautiful backgrounds bokeh when needed, even when you hold the camera to shoot. Floating focus mechanisms ensure that you achieve constantly superior optical performances at every focusing distance.

F-number: 4/Shutter speed: 1/100sec.

SEL50M28

This multipurpose 50mm "normal" macro prime lenses for full-framed sensors can be used for day-to-day photography alongside shooting outstanding 1:1 macro pictures. with this lens, you'll be able to get within 6.3" of your subject whereas its normal viewing angle allows you to include backgrounds elements for increased creative freedom. Operations and controls are enhanced for efficient, easy closeup shooting.

Focal length: 30mm/F-number: 4.0/Shutter speed: 1/500sec.

SEL30M35

This lens gives you multipurpose, high-end macro functionalities in a lightweight, compact body. It's a real 1:1 macro lens having a 2.4cm minimal working distance which allows tiny details and subjects to be rendered with impressive contrast and resolution.

Let small items play the major role

To enhance the cuteness, coolness, or characteristics of small items, it's essential to accurately focus on that item and allow it take the center stage in the shoot. This chapter offers some shooting procedures suited for tabletop photography and capturing fancy goods.

Before you start shooting, first, set your camera to **P**-mode.

Basic rule: Get very close and use the telephoto end to shoot

Whenever you shoot small items as the major subject, you can emphasize your subjects by defocusing the backgrounds. To capture closeups of subjects while defocusing other regions, the major rules are "Get very close to your subjects" and "Use the telephoto end (with lengthier focal lengths) of zoom lenses" as recommended in earlier subtopics. Nevertheless, the attributes of small items might not be effectively conveyed when you fill your whole screen with the subjects. In such instances, repeatedly shoot several shots while getting far from your subjects bit by bit.

This picture was captured using zoom lenses "SEL1855" supplied alongside NEX-F3 zoom lenses kit. Focal lengths were set at the telephoto side, 55mm, in order to defocus its backgrounds. When you focus on small items and shoot from a similar level as your subjects, the items are highlighted and their backgrounds defocused.

Additionally, macro lenses come in handy when capturing tiny items. As against other lenses, you can get extremely close to your subjects with macro lenses. Due to this, you can capture closeup shots of tiny pieces of jewellery, such as earrings, necklaces, and rings.

Lens: SEL1855/Focal length: 55mm/F-number: 5.6/ Shutter speed: 1/100sec.

This pendant was shot using macro lenses. Alongside its ability to capture closeup shots, macro lenses additionally have the immense advantage of letting photographers get very close to their subjects. With macro lenses, you have the ability to choose the size, composition, and angle of your subjects, even in limited spaces, like in small rooms or on tables.

Lens: SAL100M28/Focal length: 100mm/F-number: 7.1/Shutter
speed: 1/13sec

Considering Composition

Check out the composition before you release the shutter.
If a newbie photographer unintentionally lets go of the shutter, the
major subject is mostly placed at the middle of the frame. However,
when you're shooting small items, it tends to be a bit problematic
to use that space for photographic expressions alongside sense of
rhythms.

For capturing small subjects, it is recommended that you use
diagonal compositions or the "Rule-of-Thirds".

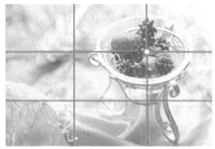

Focal length: 100mm/F-number: 2.8/Shutter speed: 1/60sec. "Rule-of-Thirds" composition

Here is an instance of "Rule-of-Thirds" compositions. Under "Rule-of-Thirds" compositions, frames are split into 9 segments (3vertical by 3horizontal), and the major subjects are positioned at intersections of dividing lines. In the instance above, the major small object is positioned at the top-right intersection.

When the major subject is positioned this way, the picture appears more stable, with perfect balances generated by the patterns of cloths on open spaces. However, when the "Rule-of-Thirds" composition is used for every shot, your pictures might become monotonous. Due to this, it is advised that you only use this composition as reference whenever you're confused about composition.

Focal length: 30mm/F-number: 3.5/Shutter speed: 1/20sec
Diagonal composition

Diagonal composition is another ideal composition for capturing small subjects. As seen in the picture above, if you line up similar patterns or items successively, and/or there are striped patterns, organize them diagonally within the frame to form the composition.

Diagonal compositions add sense of rhythms and allows viewers picture how that scene extends outside its frame.

Diagonal composition

Focal length: 18mm/F-number: 3.5/Shutter speed: 1/400sec

This picture is likewise an instance of diagonal compositions. Vibrant macaroons are rhythmically organized within the frame. This way, diagonal compositions produce perspective and rhythm, but it might give uneasy and imbalanced impressions. Rather than just using one composition, you could try different compositions. With the other instance of macaroons, you can create interesting pictures when you shoot from right above those macaroons.

Trying out macro lenses

If you regularly shoot small flowers or items, macro lenses are a must-have to boost your photographic expressions. When using macro lenses your first time, it is recommended that you use "SEL30M35" for E-mounts. They offer excellent performance at that cost and have convenient viewing angles.

Focal length: 90mm/F-number: 3.5/Shutter speed: 1/3sec.

SEL90M28G

The first E-mounts medium telephotos macro lens with inbuilt images stabilization offers impressive G-Lens quality: Stunning resolutions at about 1:1 magnification, alongside gorgeous backgrounds bokeh when needed, even with handheld shooting. Floating focus mechanisms ensures that you achieve constantly superior optical performances at every focusing distance.

F-number: 2.8/Shutter speed: 1/200sec.

SEL50M28

This multipurpose 50mm "normal" macro prime lenses for full-framed sensors is handy for day-to-day photography alongside shooting outstanding 1:1 macro pictures. It allows you get within 6.3" of your subjects whereas its normal viewing angle allows you add backgrounds element for increased creative freedom.

Operation and control are enhanced for convenient, efficient closeup shooting.

Focal length: 30mm/F-number: 3.5/Shutter speed: 1/60sec.

SEL30M35

This lens provides multipurpose, high-end macro functionalities in a lightweight, compact body. It's a rea; 1:1 macro lens having a 2.4cm minimal working distance that lets you render tiny details and subjects with excellent contrast and resolution.

Transform familiar scenes to artworks

If you enjoy shooting everyday scenes, you might discover that captured scenes appear less interesting than you expected, unable to communicate the feel of the real scenes. Here, you'll learn certain tips and functions for shooting impressive pictures of familiar scenes.

Considering composition & cropping

When taking snapshots, it is fun to take casual shots without any specific purpose. However, let us check out the compositions as well as how to crop scenes. We'll check out how to go about cropping scenes first. When you simply take your camera out and begin shooting, the picture often appears cluttered with undesirable objects added to the frame.

 Rather than trying to get everything into your frame, only focus focus on the major subject, particularly when taking casual shots of everyday scenes.

Generally, a focal length (viewing angle) similar to that of the human visual range can be selected by slightly moving zoom position towards the telephoto end. Zoom should be used actively when shooting snapshots.

Focal length: 35mm/F-number: 5.6/Shutter speed:
1/1000sec/Exposure compensation: +1/White balance:
Shade/Creative Style: Landscape (Contrast: +3, Saturation: -3)

Captured with normal zoom lenses SEL1855 at focal lengths of 35mm, this picture cropped your scene having the flag as the major subject. When you slightly move zoom position towards the telephoto end, it ensures optimum balance between the flag's size as well as the depth and size of the buildings around it.

Focal length: 23mm

This picture was captured using the wide-angled end, attempting to add lots of objects, like the street lamps and the buildings. Due to this, the largest region within the frame is filled by the ground and the buildings, and the crucial flag only appears in a tiny size at the back. Contrasted with this picture, the first shot, which used the telephoto end to capture the flag appears more outstanding.

Focal length: 50mm/F-number: 8.0/Shutter speed: 1/250sec. Focal length: 50mm/F-number: 8.0/Shutter speed: 1/1000sec.

Both examples above were captured at focal lengths of 50mm. This type of dramatic cropping can likewise make certain scenes interesting.

These are closeups of scenes captured using telephoto zoom lenses while walking along the street. When you capture small parts of scenes tightly in the frames, it inspires viewers to imagine atmospheres that can't be seen within the picture.

There are general kinds of photographic compositions, like
diagonal compositions and the "Rule-of-Thirds". However, if you
are extremely conscious of these types of compositions, your
pictures will become uninteresting and lose personality. They
should only be kept as references for when you're confused about
composition. Rather, discover your preferred expression or
composition, particularly when you're walking around or going on
casual outings. Take pictures that you enjoy; that's what counts
when creating your own artworks.

If you're able to fully use zoom, you'll find it easy to crop everyday
scenes to generate outstanding artworks. Though you might be
unable to get your expected result in the first few tries, be
intentional about using zoom and get your own feel.

Focal length: 11mm/F-number: 5.6/Shutter speed: 1/160sec.

Using Picture Effects

To add distinct finishes to your pictures, try out the Picture Effects function. When you use Picture Effects, you can conveniently shoot artistic pictures like paintings or retro-style pictures without using your computer to retouch them. (*) α-cameras have different effects, and here are some instances.

Kinds of available effects in Picture Effects differ based on your camera model.

High Contrast Monochromes allow you capture high-contrast monochrome pictures as though they were captured using black-and-white film. It's most ideal for powerfully rendering streets. Additionally, in scenarios where color pictures don't appear quite impressive, like on cloudy or rainy days, simply using this effect turns your pictures into works of art.

High Contrast Monochromes

Soft High-key allows you capture pale and soft pictures with slight blue casts. Irrespective of your subject, it adds fantasy-like or pleasant finishes to the picture.

Soft High-key

Partial Color generates images that retain specific colors and changes other colors into black-and-white. When you use this effect, even pictures of laundries will become stylish works of art. When this is used on small items and flowers, it also creates impressive artworks.

Partial Colors (Blue)

There are different effects asides these, such as "Posterization (Color)", "Retro Photo", "Miniature" and "Toy Camera". Try out different effects for capturing casual everyday scenes.

Toy Camera

Miniature

Retro Photo

Trying out fixed focal lengths lenses

Since fixed focal lengths lenses generate impressive backgrounds defocus, they're able to turn shots of familiar landscapes or your snapshots into distinct artworks. Additionally, since they allow large amounts of light into the camera, they're handy for indoor shoots or shots of a street at night.

Focal length: 35mm/F-number: 1.8/Shutter speed: 1/80sec.

SEL35F18F

Offers impressive picture quality even at maximum apertures of F1.8. This is a lightweight and compact 35mm prime lens for full-framed cameras and is a multipurpose choice for all types of shoots ranging from table top pictures to outdoor shoots. Quiet, precise, fast AF operations and trustworthy AF tracking makes it ideal for shooting stills and videos.

Focal length: 50mm/F-number: 1.8/Shutter speed: 1/3200sec.

SEL50F18F

Large apertures 50mm prime lenses are compulsory for professional full-framed camera users; this particular one is an affordable and excellent choice. It has a state-of-the-art optical design for high picture quality, and its large maximum aperture of

F1.8 produces beautiful backgrounds bokeh. With APS-C formats E-mounts bodies, you'll get equally high image quality with equivalent focal lengths of approximately 75mm.

Shoot cityscapes when traveling

You can capture cityscapes that are alien to your everyday life. Here, you will be provided with certain techniques that capture the feel of those types of cityscapes in pictures.

First, set your camera to A-mode to enable you alter aperture and capture using smaller apertures (about F8 if you're shooting during the day).

Considering compositions and how to go about cropping

To be able to capture the feel of the cityscape, first consider the composition. In casual shots when traveling, we tend to use the wide-angled end (has a shorter focal length) to shoot, in an attempt to fill the frame with as many items as possible. However, based on a scene, shooting with the telephoto end (has a longer focal length) best conveys the atmosphere. Below are some examples of this effect.

[1] Focal length: 16mm/F-number: 10/Shutter speed: 1/100sec. [2]
Focal length: 16mm/F-number: 5.6/Shutter speed: 1/160sec.

These pictures were captured at 16mm, using the wide-angled end of normal zoom lenses.

In picture [1], it emphasizes the building. Nevertheless, since a building fills the largest region of your frame, the picture doesn't properly communicate the actual feel of the cityscape. As seen in the example above, when the wide-angled end is used in shooting, objects on the foregrounds appear large, whereas objects on the backgrounds look smaller than they really are. This composition is handy for just highlighting a building and causing it to appear powerful. However, if your goal is to shoot the whole feel of the streets and city, use a different composition.

In picture [2], which was also captured using the wide-angled end, the largest region is filled by the ground and the building. However, due to "radial composition", with the street's end at the middle of your frame, this picture has increased depth as against picture [1]. If you'd rather shoot such pictures, then consider how the street is facing when shooting.

Now, we will consider how it alters the impression when the telephoto end is used in shooting.

Focal length: 50mm/F-number: 8.0/Shutter speed: 1/80sec.

This picture is captured at 50mm of zoom lenses. To focus on the background and foreground, aperture values was set at F8. Additionally, to stop buildings from looking tilted and making the picture appear unstable, the camera was held securely in a vertical position.

Shot using the telephoto end, the picture successfully records the attributes of the cityscape. As against the picture captured using the wide-angled end, the building towards the near end doesn't fill a large region. Additionally, the street fills ¼th of the whole frame. Such compositions give natural perspectives to the picture.

Focal length: 50mm/F-number: 6.3/Shutter speed: 1/80sec.

This picture was also captured at 50mm. Even in these types of scenes where cloudy skies could take up the most part of the frame if captured with the wide-angled end, the cityscapes are captured with viewing angles similar to that of the human eye by using the telephoto end to shoot.

Focal length: 30mm/F-number: 7.1/Shutter speed: 1/60sec/ISO: 160

This method of cropping parts of scenes with the telephoto end is likewise handy for taking shots from vantage spots, alongside shooting streets.

[1] Focal length: 28mm/F-number: 8.0/Shutter speed: 1/160sec/ISO: 200 [2] Focal length: 135mm/F-number: 8.0/Shutter speed: 2.5sec.

When viewing vistas from vantage points, we majorly tend to use the wide-angled end to capture the whole landscape. Nevertheless, when you crop portions of the landscapes into the frames, you can

132

capture pictures that will be more effective at communicating the distinct feel of the cityscape.

Picture [1] was captured at 28mm, with zoom positions slightly moved towards the telephoto end with regular zoom lenses. From the whole city spreading outside the frame, this frame only captures the most outstanding parts. In picture [2], boldly shot at 135mm, the whole frame is occupied with houses. With every house rendered with its proper dimension, this is likewise an impressive picture that communicates the atmosphere.

This way, you can effectively convey the atmospheres of cityscapes by using the telephoto end to crop distinctive parts into your frame. Fully use the zoom lenses by trying out different focal lengths.

Trying out high magnifications zoom lenses

Lenses labelled as "high magnifications zoom lenses" are handy for travel. Because high magnifications zoom lenses ranges from wide-angled to telephoto all by itself, it is able to take outstanding pictures of a travel scene using different expressions. Additionally, since you won't have to change lenses for every scene, the chances of you missing shooting opportunities are low, leaving you to concentrate on living your best life during your trip.

F-number: 6.3/Shutter speed: 1/125sec.

SEL24240

A 24mm to 240mm 10x zoom ranges lets this individual lens to span extensive varieties of shooting scenarios, making it the go-to lens for travels where the goal is to minimize luggage alongside for shooting portraits, snapshots, architecture, landscapes and lots more.

Alternate between telephoto and wide-angled without having to switch lenses, allowing you shoot more of these passing moments. With its advanced optics, aberration is effectively subdued while attaining high resolutions all through the picture area, and precision linear motors drive focus for smooth, quick response.

Handheld telephotos pictures and low-light photography are enhanced by inbuilt OSS (Optical SteadyShot) images stabilization, and its design is moisture and sut resistant for trustworthy operations in extreme conditions.

Focal length: 28mm/F-number: 10/Shutter speed: 20sec.

SEL18200LE

Significantly lighter and smaller than other lenses, this is the perfect lens for wide ranges of shooting scenarios. The lens' wide focal lengths coverage, from 18mm to 200mm (27mm to 300mm in 35mm equivalent), makes it the must have high magnifications "travel" lens. Blur resulting from camera shake whenever you're shooting with lengthier focal lengths or in dark environments are reduced by Optical SteadyShots technology.

Capture Motion in Pictures

Here, we will discuss certain techniques for shooting mobile subjects in sports scenarios and/or railway photography conveying an atmosphere of dynamism and presence. α-cameras are fitted with different functions for capturing mobile subjects. For your first attempt, use the advice given below.

Shooting with motion stopped

You can momentarily stop a subject's motion and shoot it as an outstanding best shot when you use a faster shutter speed to shoot. You can set shutter speed to your preference in **S**-mode, however, first make use of "Sports Action" modes under Scenes Selections (shooting mode).

"Sports Action" modes let you capture shots where the motion of mobile subjects is frozen. With AF operation and a faster shutter speed to continually track the motion of subjects, this is the ideal mode for mobile subjects. Additionally, as this mode automatically activates continuous shooting modes, it's easier to shoot the best moments of the scenes. Bear in mind that continuous shooting ends when you release the shutter once. Ensure you hold the shutter tab down throughout the scene you'll like to capture.

1/800sec.   1/800sec.

137

To capture the examples above, the photographer presses and holds the shutter tab down while the dog is running. The 2 pictures above are outstanding shots amongst the continuous shots. When you set shutter speed to 1/800sec, the subject's motion appears stopped.

Since the "Sports Actions" mode under Scenes Selections is one of many automatic shooting modes, you can't adjust the settings for color and brightness. In order to change them using the functions, such as white balance and exposure compensation, use **S**-mode to shoot. When you use S-mode, select Continuous AF (AF-C) as autofocus mode and Continuous Shooting as drive mode, such that you're able to continuously shoot subjects.

Deciding composition

Once you're accustomed to continuous shooting, also note the composition. As displayed in preceding subtopics, the "Rule-of-Thirds" composition is the ideal well-balanced composition. However, when you'll like to convey the dynamisms of a scene, it is recommended that you go for compositions that position subjects at the middle of a frame.

This composition comes in handy for clearly expressing the theme and power of subjects. When capturing sports scenes, when you capture closeups of the major subjects in motion at the middle of a frame, you'll be able to finish your pictures up impressively fully conveying the presence.

Focal length: 300mm/F-number: 5.6/Shutter speed: 1/2500sec.

The examples above are captured using compositions with subjects at the middle of the frames. When you use telephotos lens to zoom in on subjects, the pictures communicate the dynamism and power of subjects. Additionally, with subjects at the middle of frames, it's easier to focus on them.

Whenever you're shooting mobile subjects, the scenario can dramatically change in moments, unlike when capturing stationary landscapes. Hence, you should prioritize shooting as much shots as you can and never missing shooting opportunities. First, be accustomed to continuous shooting and let the composition be till you have additional leeway. You could also compose pictures by using a computer to trim them once you're home.

Focal length: 70mm/F-number: 5.6/Shutter speed: 1/400sec.

Trying out telephoto lenses

In sports environments like the examples above, you can effectively convey dynamism when you zoom in on subjects. Particularly, in environments where shooting is to be done from afar, it is best that you use telephoto lenses. For individuals whose interest lie along shooting animals, birds, and sports games, telephoto lenses come in handy.

Lens focal lengths: 200mm/F-number: 6.3/Shutter speed: 1/2000sec.

SEL200600G

Ideal for wildlife photography and lots more, this 200mm to 600mm super-telephotos zoom reaches as far as 1200mm or 840mm with 2.0x and 1.4x teleconverters, fitted with AF performance and full G-lens quality. ED and aspherical glass elements attain impressive resolutions all through a zoom range, whereas Sony's Nano AR Coatings eliminates ghosting and flare. Its bokeh is also gorgeous.

F-number: 16/Shutter speed: 1/6sec.

SEL70300G

The first full-framed 70mm to 300mm E-mounts zoom offers impressive image-wide resolutions. It likewise allows you get within distance of subjects for impressive details and closeups with minimum focus of 2.95-feet. Its inbuilt Optical SteadyShot images stabilization effectively counteracts camera shake resulting from close focus to telephotos, whereas advanced linear actuators ensure fast, accurate autofocus. It is also resistant to moisture and dust.

Lens focal lengths: 193mm/F-number: 6.3/Shutter speed: 1/50sec.

SEL70350G

Optimized mechanical and optical design offers impressive super-telephotos zoom performances for APS-C bodies (equivalent to 105mm to 525mm). It maintains outstanding G-Lens quality all through the zoom ranges right towards the edges of the image. All this is fitted into this compact, 5x mobile super-telephotos zoom lenses with inbuilt optical images stabilization.

Focal length: 208mm/F-number: 6.3/Shutter speed: 1/320sec.

SEL55210

This is 3.8x zoom lenses goes from 55mm right out to 210mm with constantly impressive optical performance every step of the way. Due to its Optical SteadyShot images stabilization, it is easier to attain sharp, stable videos and images in low lighting or when you're zooming-in on subjects that are farther away. Additionally, internal focusing and internal drives motor make responsive and smooth AF possible with minimal noise, ideal for video capture.

Capturing Gorgeous Party Photos

Poor lighting makes it hard to shoot beautiful pictures of indoor celebrations and parties in a dim environment. Here, we consider certain techniques for shooting whatever you see.

Capturing Whatever You See

Whenever you are shooting indoors under low lighting, the inbuilt flash fires of your camera prevent blurring. However, whenever the flash light directly lights your subjects up, the light is able to reflect in a way that makes the surrounding region appear a bit underexposed, making the picture appear unnatural as seen below.

Illuminated with flash

Not illuminated with flash

First, let us attempt shooting without making use of the inbuilt flash. Begin by choosing **Anti Motion Blurs*** under Scenes Selections. Under Anti Motion Blurs mode, 6 pictures are continuously shot every time you release the shutter, and these pictures are superimposed – one above the other, to minimize noise. Areas with minimal noise can be captured (as against using Intelligent Auto to shoot), and fast shutter speeds and high sensitivities are set. Additionally, mobile subjects and their backgrounds are detected and superimposed, one above the other, to enable you shoot while regulating subject blur and camera shake.

This might be located in another place apart from Scenes Selections, based on the specific camera you are using.

Capturing one photo (subject blur)

Anti Motion Blur mode

However, since Anti Motion Blurs mode happens to be an automatic capture mode, you cannot set the brightness and color tone as discussed in the following section. To alter those attributes using exposure compensations and white balance functions, use **A**-mode to shoot. When **A**-mode is used in shooting, the aperture should be opened very wide. Should blurring still happen, shoot while you manually increase the sensitivity.

The above section discusses how to take shots without making use of the flash. Should blurring still happen when you use this method, make use of the flash. Switch to **P**-mode whenever you're doing this, to enable you alter the brightness and color tone as discussed in the following section.

Adjusting Color Tone

Color tones is essential to shooting whatever you see and you can adjust it via the white-balance function. First, let us use the **AWB** white-balance settings to shoot. With auto white-balance (AWB), your camera automatically alters color tone in accordance with the scene, though at times the color tone so determined by auto white balance doesn't fit match how the scene appears to the human eye. When this occurs, fine-tune white balance. Whenever you are taking shots under warm-colored lightings, try altering white balance towards A (amber) to convey the warmth that's visible to the human eye.

Image appears bluer than what the naked eye sees

White balance adjusted toward amber

When Subjects Aren't in Focus

The camera is delivered with AF (autofocus) function for automatically focusing on subjects, though AF can be minimally ideal for scenes that are dim and poorly lit. In this instance, you could use any one of the solutions below.

AF Lock

With AF, it is easier to focus on strongly contrasted or bright objects. So whenever your desired subject isn't in focus, check for brighter objects, like objects or food under spotlights. The idea is to check for objects that are similar distances away from your camera as the subjects to be captured. Once you discover bright locations, point your camera towards them, alter AF, point your camera again towards the subjects to be captured while retaining AF, compose your shot, and touch the shutter tab to shoot.

Under default settings, a half-touch of shutter tab activates AF, as a result, direct your camera towards bright locations, half-push the shutter tab, and immediately you achieve focus, compose your shot while you keep half-pressing the shutter tab.

MF (Manual Focus)

Another method is to focus on your desired subjects using manual focus. When you choose **MF**, you can manually alter focus by rotating the lens' focus rings. However, focus adjustment and camera settings with manual focus take a while to get accustomed to. If you're planning to use MF in your shoots, then practice MF beforehand. Additionally, the way to change between AF and MF differs based on the model of your camera.

Using External Flashes

Though we have considered various shooting methods that don't make use of flash, you'll be able to shoot more gorgeous pictures conveying the atmosphere of the scenes using bounce flashes photography with optional external flashes.

Bounce flashes photography entails illuminating subjects with indirect lighting that gets bounced off walls or ceilings. Such light is softly diffused, giving off a very natural picture by minimizing unnatural shadows as well as shines on faces which majorly occurs whenever the inbuilt flash is used in illuminating subjects directly.

Directly illuminating the face with a flash

HVL-F60RM

The HVL-F60RM clip-ons flash units feature high GN60 power, supports fast operation and high speed continuous shooting and is suitable for advanced as well as professional photographers. It also comprises wireless radio receivers/commanders.

Bounce flash photography with external flash

HVL-F45RM

Supplies intense lighting with its compact high-end HVL-F45RM clip-ons flashes. Experience the freedom that inbuilt wireless radio controls under multi-flash settings as well as conventional optical wireless communications. It can be operated easily, has excellent reliability, and produces expert results particularly for advocates of compacts α E-mounts interchangeable-lenses cameras.

The usability of the available external flash differs in accordance with the model of the camera used. Ensure that an external flash is supported by your camera model before you go ahead to purchase the equipment.

Photographing Night Skies

If you have ever desired to capture the star-filled night sky, here is an opportunity to do just that. With the ideal technique, your camera will be able to capture myriad sources of light above. Below are some beginner-friendly techniques for creating spectacular pictures of stars.

Preparing to Capture Pictures of Stars

Choose the right surrounding is the first step to capturing beautiful pictures of the sky at night. In big urban regions, light pollution (artificial night time lights) illuminate the sky at night, making the stars almost invisible. For impressive pictures of the stars, it is best to shoot from mountains or high elevations with minimal light pollutions and clear skies, though you could also attempt shooting from nearby parks without the visible city light.

Where capturing the stars is concerned, moonlight is also considered as light pollution. We advise that you shoot during new moons or after the setting of the moon.

You must keep the shutter open for extended periods to capture the stars, so it's best you hold the camera in place with tripod as though you're capturing night scenes. Though remotes commanders are crucial whenever you use tripods to shoot, you can likewise set self-timers to 2 seconds if there isn't a tripod. This helps in preventing blurring resulting from vibrations whenever you press the shutter tab. Additionally, when you use tripod, ensure you deactivate the images stabilization functions to avoid malfunctions.

Configuring the Settings of the Camera

After securing your camera to tripod, configure its settings. There are different ways to capture the sky at night, including shooting the stars as they appear, capturing time-lapse images where the stars are in motion, as well as using telephotos settings to capture nebulas.

First, we'll check out the most convenient method: how to shoot still images of the stars.

If you're using zoom lenses, make use of the wide-angled settings (shortest focal lengths). This allows you to shoot more scenery and stars simultaneously.

Wide-angled imaged of scenery and night sky.

Images of star trails.

Next, set **M**-mode under capture modes, and alter the sensitivity, shutter speed, and aperture.

1. Aperture

Open aperture very wide during shoots to get more light and also ease the process of photographing the stars.

2. Shutter speed

Though shutter speed is dependent on the particular lens in use, you could try to set it to about 8 seconds. Unlike fixed scenes shot using tripods, stars are always on the move though at slow paces. Hence, should the shutter be extremely long, the stars would have the appearance of lines within u=images, making it difficult to clearly capture them.

3. Sensitivity

You cannot easily determine the ideal sensitivity since it greatly varies in accordance with the degree of moonlight and light pollution, the particular lens in use, the day and shooting location. First use ISO400 to shoot, and afterwards get the ideal value by observing the outcomes of the shoot.

Once you have configured all three settings above, you are all set to begin shooting stars, but first ensure you adjust your focus on the stars. AF (Autofocus) doesn't function under dim settings like night skies, so adjust MF (manual focus). It can be quite difficult to adjust focus on small stars while looking at LCD screens, as a result, you can use MF Assist and Focus Magnifier functions to really focus on the bright stars exactly as they look enlarged on your monitor. The operation tabs can be used in moving the magnified area, to enable you look for luminous stars which you can focus on.

Monitor views sans Focus Magnifier (an example).

Monitor views alongside Focus Magnifier (an example).

Whenever you find bright stars, rotate the focus rings till the star's outline is defined. The star might be out of focus since the focus rings were turned towards the farthest end (infinity), so we advise that you magnify the display in order to confirm the focus. When the display goes entirely dark making it difficult to see the scenery and stars, increase sensitivity to ISO3200 or IOS6400 to increase the visibility of the images on your display, and give it another try. Immediately the stars come into focus, apply caution so that the focus doesn't get adjusted till you finish shooting. Focus positions might change if you select **AF** or change the lens' zoom positions.

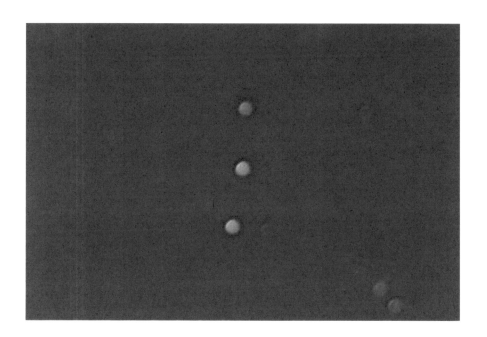

If focus is not correct, stars look blurry.

Check the Outcomes While Shooting

Once your star comes into focus, push the shutter tab to capture a shot. Noise reductions operate for some seconds after taking your shot, as a result, it might take a while before the monitor displays the picture.

Enlarge the picture and check out the outcome. Did you shoot the stars?
Shooting using the settings above captures stars as seen below.

Focal length: 19mm, f-stop: 3.5, Shutter speed: 5seconds.

Parts of Orion constellations enlarged on a playback screen. The
stars are shot as spots of light.

If the whole picture is extremely dark or extremely bright, shoot
several pictures using different shutter speed and sensitivity
settings. The brightness of the image increases with increase in
sensitivity, and you'll be able to shoot images at very fast shutter

speeds, though should the sensitivity happen to be extremely high, the picture might contain noise and its resolutions could also be degraded. Additionally, when the monitor gets extremely bright, you might be unable to correctly ascertain the image's brightness. Whenever you're shooting in dim locations, we advise that you set the monitor's brightness way lower than you set it when you use it in the day.

When the stars don't get captured as seen with the human eye, check back with the pictures on your playback screen to determine if they're too dark, too bright, or out-of-focus, and take another shot.
It's also likely that the night sky became cloudier between the time you last looked at it and the time you captured it.

Adjust the Color and Composition

After you have ascertained that you're able to shoot the stars, you could attempt adjusting the color and composition. Capturing the stars alongside the surrounding landscape makes for an impressive shot. Check out your environment and try adding distant views or trees into your compositions. When changing compositions, apply caution so that you don't move the already adjusted focus ring.

Using the white-balance function, you can alter color in accordance with your taste though you can choose **Fluor: Warm White** or **Incandescent**, for instance, to create clear images of bluish starry skies. You can likewise choose Auto WB (**AWB**) for very natural palettes similar to that seen with the human eye.

Auto white-balance   **Incandescent** white-balance

Commercially obtainable soft filters come in handy for emphasizing the stars by softly blurring their star lights. With this, you can shoot larger pictures of stars, you could even use wide-angled lenses for this.

Photo captured with soft filters on a lens.

Lens focal lengths: 24mm/F-number: 1.4/Shutter speed: 8sec.

SEL24F14GM

Unsparing applications of advanced technologies achieves G-Master performances with constantly high resolutions and gentle, natural bokeh even at its broadest F1.4 apertures setting. This lens is quite compact and very light in its league, with emphasis on portability. Additionally, it offers fast, accurate AF drive, reliability and advanced control.

Photographing Fireworks Displays

Fireworks are great in the summer. With your camera, you'll be able to shoot mesmerizing pictures of fireworks illuminating the night skies for bright, passing moments. Ready to capture snapshots of fireworks this summer?

Getting Set to Shoot Pictures of Fireworks

To capture captivating pictures of fireworks shooting above, you'll need to hold your camera in place using a tripod, since the shutter must be kept open for extended periods. You'll also need remote commanders to open the camera's shutter at exactly the perfect time. Asides having the right tool when capturing fireworks, the location of your shoot also matters. Position yourself in the central viewing area to be able to listen to announcements as they are being made, to also be closer to the action that you desire to capture as well as also experience the feel of the firework display. Whenever you're taking your shot from this section, be careful so that you don't obstruct the views of those around you. With very tall tripods, lower its length without stretching out its leg so as not to obstruct those behind you as well as avoid blurring resulting from wind and vibration. Ensure to check beforehand that tripods are allowed within the premises.

The kind of remotes commanders to be used are dependent on the model of your camera.

On the D-day, go a bit early to the venue so that you can set your equipment up while the day is still bright. Additionally, it's crucial that you confirm that there aren't any electrical lines or street lights that might obstruct you during the shoot.

The specific lens t eb used varies in accordance with the kind of picture you'll like to shoot as well as how far you are from the launch section, however, we advise that you use standard zoom lenses provided in the lens kit. This lens allows you capture very expansive wide-angled shots using short focal lengths (1) and extremely detailed telephotos shots using long focal lengths (2).

(1) Focal lengths: 20mm.   (2) Focal lengths: 70mm.

Picture taken from afar using telephotos setting.

Configuring the Settings of your Camera

After setting up the equipment, configure the settings of the camera.

Select **M**-mode under capture modes on your camera, and afterwards set the shutter speed, aperture, and sensitivity.

1. Sensitivity

Fireworks are extremely bright, so it's best to shoot sensitivity set as ISO100. You can use the aperture to make up for the brilliance of the fireworks.

2. Aperture (f-stop)

Although the perfect f-stop differs in accordance with the kind of fireworks, many kinds of fireworks can be shot with suitable exposure when you use f-stops of f13. When it happens that the captured firework trail is either extremely bright or extremely dark, use f-stops in the ranges of f10 through f18 as your standard. Though the f-stop is best fine-tuned in accordance with the kind of fireworks, we advise that you fix f-stop and keep focusing on shutter speed till you get accustomed to it.

3. Shutter speed

When you know the duration for which the shutter is to be kept open, you are well on your way to shooting impressive pictures of fireworks. For shutter speeds, choose **BULB** to enable you manually alter the duration for which you keep the shutter open. Once the fireworks are launched, open your camera's shutter and leave it open till all the fireworks have vanished. You'll be able to shoot beautiful images of fireworks trails as displayed in (1). When you choose a very fast shutter speed, it would display the fireworks as dots, see (2) below.

Also, since you must configure your camera to release shutter using remotes commander, ensure to check the settings method beforehand, which differs in accordance with the model of your camera. Check the Handbook or User Manual for details. **BULB** can still be used to release shutter without using remotes commander but apply caution since vibrations from touching the shutter release tab could result in camera shake as well as blurry images.

Whichever way, ensure to deactivate the SteadyShot and Long Exposures NR functions.

(1) Shutter speeds: 4seconds.   (2) Shutter speeds: 1/100seconds.

While opening the shutter all through the series of continuous fireworks shots creates gorgeous images, light from different fireworks could overlap at one particular spot, resulting in images with white, overexposed regions.

Several bursts' fireworks overlapped.

Now You Are All Set to Shoot

Now that you have set the equipment up and configured the settings on your camera, you're all set to shoot. First, adjust the focus of your camera on the firework.

Using manual focus, you can alter the focus on the real fireworks. Since it can be quite difficult to alter focus with the first burst from the fireworks, you can make use of the first multiple displays of fireworks in adjusting focus, and afterwards prepare yourself for both the middle and ending of the show.

For detailed focusing, it's best to make use of the Focus Magnifier and MF Assist functions.

If you're not accustomed to MF, you could focus on those fireworks using autofocus, and afterwards immediately switch again to MF. Either way, you can enlarge captured pictures on your playback screen to ascertain if subjects are in focus.

Once you have focused on the fireworks, you can keep shooting using that same focus point, which might change whenever you zoom out or in or change the compositions. When this happens, we advise that you check out the focus on the captured pictures.

Magnify portions of fireworks on your playback screen.

White-balance plays an important role in capturing pictures of fireworks comprising the same brilliant colors that you can see. While AWB can be used in capturing beautiful colors, for a more realistic color, try using Incandescent to shoot fireworks using intermediate colors, like lemon yellow, pink, and cyan; you can also capture fireworks made up primarily of orange when you use Daylight.

For more vibrant pictures, use Creative Look/Creative Style and afterwards adjust saturations to higher values to generate more vibrant pictures.

AWB white-balance.

Incandescent white-balance.

Higher saturation.

When pictures seem whitish or their colors appear dull in spite of adjusting saturation and white balance, the picture might be overexposed. When this happens, close aperture a little and try shooting again.

Once you're accustomed to the photography, adjust the compositions to match the fireworks.

Though the best composition is dependent on the particular lens you are using, the picture you are trying to capture, and your shooting location, if you'll like to shoot individual bursts of firework, use vertical compositions whereas to shoot wide fireworks bursts, like those that normally take place during grand finales, use horizontal compositions to fill images with fireworks. Additionally, you can likewise capture images with horizontal positions when shooting individual bursts alongside background sceneries.

Vertical shot.

Horizontal shots of wide fireworks bursts.

Using Remote Commanders

To use **BULB** mode to shoot fireworks, you'll need remote commanders. When you use remote commanders under **BULB** modes, you can personalize the numbers of bursts as well as the fireworks trails within one picture. Since the shutter can be released whenever you want without having to look at your camera, you don't have to stay in place watching the camera; you can also enjoy the display.

Additionally, the use of remote commanders minimizes blurry pictures resulting from camera shake brought about when you released the shutter and also permits long exposures of over thirty seconds, which comes in handy whenever you're using tripods for night sky and night time photography.

Available remotes commanders differ in accordance with the model of your camera. Before purchase, confirm if the remotes commander (RM-VPR1, RMT-P1BT) is compatible with your camera.

Shutter speed: 37seconds.

RMT-P1BT

RM-VPR1

This remotes commander has several terminals. It allows remote operations of shutter lock (bulb) and zoom and is supplied with cables for shooting movies and still images.

Photographing Colors of Autumn Foliage

You could try out certain shooting techniques to enable you shoot the beauties of trees covered in yellows and reds. When capturing autumn foliage, your camera must be set to **A**-mode so that you can personalize aperture. In general, if your goal is to capture the whole scene, minimize aperture, however, if the plan is to shoot closeups of branches or leaves, open aperture to the fullest.

Consider the Light's Direction

Before setting up your camera, we'll consider how to use the light to your advantage. When capturing autumn colors, the resultant picture greatly differs based om the weather, specific time of the day as well as the direction light is coming from.

On clear days, you can generally divide light direction into back light, side light and front light.

With front light, the light falls on subjects as viewed from the camera. Front light allows you capture colourful pictures that look as natural as when seen with the human eye. However, since there aren't any shadows, the resultant picture appears ordinary without any depth to it.

Front light

Shooting using front light.

Focal lengths: 35mm, f-stop: 10.0, Shutter speeds: 1/50second.

Side light

As can be deduced from its name, this light falls sideways on subjects. When you use side light in shooting, it emphasizes shadows on trees to add depth to the landscape. If you're taking shots at dusk, ensure that you use the side light in shooting your images.

Shooting using side light.

Focal lengths: 200mm, f-stops: 8.0, Shutter speeds: 1/60second.

Back light

This light hits subjects from behind. Whenever back lights shine through foliage, it enhances their vibrant colors and translucency, so they appear as though they are shining in pictures. Differences in contrast between backlit subjects and dark backgrounds express dram, so ensure you use back light to the fullest.

Whenever you use back light, saturation and image contrast can reduce if sunlight directly enters your lens. Whenever this occurs, simply adjust the camera's angle to the leaves or sunlight, such that sunlight doesn't directly enter your lens. Additionally, subjects have the tendency to darken whenever strong lights point into your lens. Whenever subjects appear dark or duller than you expected, increase exposure compensations towards the + end to achieve similar brightness as seem with the human eye.

Shooting using back light.

Focal lengths: 11mm, f-stops: 14.0, Shutter speeds: 1/30second.

Whenever back light enters your lens directly

You can use this method to capture under different kinds of light, noting the camera's position in relation to the sun. You don't have to wait till sunny days before capturing fall foliage. Different expressions can be captured on both rainy and cloudy days too. On cloudy days, colors might not be really vibrant like they appear under sunlight, however, the whole scene is covered in soft lighting, giving off an atmosphere of serenity void of undesired shadows.

Cloudy day shots.

Rainy days are also good for capturing good pictures. Under the rain, light gets increasingly softer and colors appear increasingly subdued. Additionally, dusts on leaves get washed off, while droplets of water on the leaves and ground glow moistly.

Rainy day shots.

Focal lengths: 115mm, f-stops: 11.0, Shutter speeds: 1second.

Whenever you include overcasts or rainy skies in your composition, it emphasizes the white skies, resulting in conventional-looking images. When this happens, shooting only the landscapes without adding the sky emphasizes the major autumn colors resulting in a spectacular image.

Capturing The Things You See

Shooting autumn foliage exactly as they appear needs not just the perfect light direction, but additionally needs the adjustment of color and brightness via the settings on the camera. Though the suitable color and brightness is automatically calculated by the camera, the outcome might not fit the picture you're planning to shoot or the atmosphere that you felt. When you find it difficult to shoot the scene as you see it, try modifying white balance and exposure compensation. Images that perfectly depict the scene have the appropriate brightness and color.

The needed adjustments differ in accordance with the subject, weather conditions, and light direction, and are discussed below using different examples. While shooting, make necessary adjustments while looking at the outcome on your camera monitor as you keep shooting pictures one after the other, and find your preferred image.

To use exposure compensation

Exposure compensations: 0

Exposure compensations: +2.0

When backgrounds are bright as a result of back light, foliage might appear heavy and dark. When this occurs, adjust exposure compensations towards + to enhance the foliage's vibrant colors. The background can be adjusted such that it looks a bit overexposed.

Using white-balance

Cloudy WB

You can effectively use white balance to emphasize vibrancy. When capturing images on cloudy days or in shades, setting white-balance to Cloudy increases the general reds in your picture and increases the brilliance of the yellows and reds in autumn foliage. Fine-tuning white-balance is also handy for carrying out detailed adjustments on colors.

When taking snapshots or shooting landscapes, there might be the temptation to increase saturation using Creative Look/Creative Style to further emphasize the vividness, but since autumn's foliage has an already high saturation, this might result in the color getting saturated causing the picture to lose depth, hence it isn't recommended.

Increasing saturation oversaturates reds and makes images look flat.

Rather than increase saturation, adjust the white balance and exposure compensation.

However, when it comes to colors, it is all about your preference as a person; there isn't a wrong or right choice. As displayed in the image below, you can use white balance to apply blues to shots from cloudy days to convey an atmosphere of tranquility and coldness.

Daylight White Balance on cloudy days

Shooting with several Compositions

Once you're in control of vividness and color, you could change compositions to generate different atmospheres of autumn foliage.

Different lenses for different expressions

As displayed below, the shooting method completely differs between when using wide-angled settings and telephotos settings, even for that same scenery. Wide angles result in inspiring pictures, and telephotos angles closes the distance between you and your subjects and creates blur. When you optimize pictures from different angles using different lenses, you can further enhance the properties of autumn foliage.

Wide-angled shots, Focal lengths: 18mm, f-stops: 8.0.

Telephotos angle shots, Focal lengths: 90mm, f-stops: 8.0.

Shooting from wide angles

When capturing images from wide angles (short focal lengths), wide landscapes can be fitted into images, however, you can likewise generate dynamic expressions which further emphasize height and perspective. There's also minimal blurring, which enables objects all through wide areas to stay in focus. You can fit full landscapes into view by setting aperture within the ranges of f8.0 through f11.

Focal lengths: 11mm, f-stops: 8.0, Shutter speeds: 1/25seconds.

This picture was captured using wide-angled lenses looking upwards. It places emphasis on the trees' heights stretching upwards starting at the left, resulting in an inspiring picture.

Focal lengths: 11mm, f-stops: 10.0, Shutter speeds: 1/60second.

This is a closeup shot of the vibrant autumn leaves. The way the leaves contrast against the broad background results in a dynamic picture. This way, the attributes of wide angles enhances subjects with foreground-to- background contrasts. Additionally, when you close aperture down to f10, it depicts the background well without extreme blurring.

Shooting with telephoto angles

With telephotos lenses (long focal lengths when using zoom lenses), subjects background tend to get greatly defocused, causing impressive aspects to be made to stand-out amongst the wide expanse of landscape. Telephotos lenses are likewise handing for creating compressed effects that comprises all the items within a picture without losing hold of the perspectives of mountains spread around the background as well as the sceneries on the foreground.

Focal lengths: 200mm, f-stops: 3.2, Shutter speeds: 1/80second.

Here, telephotos lenses were used in capturing autumn colors. Both the background and foreground are impressively defocused. When telephotos settings are closer-up, the focus range becomes smaller and the background gets defocused more, enhancing the pictures in the foliage. To increase blurring, open the aperture very wide while shooting.

Watch out for the colors of the backgrounds whenever you are taking this type of picture. The above picture was captured at angles such that the yellow leaves stay in the background resulting in vivid impressions in the entire picture.

Focal lengths: 160mm, f-stops: 8.0, Shutter speeds: 1/60second.

When shooting beautiful sceneries, there is the urge to attempt to capture everything in one picture. If you have ever shot images that failed to convey the atmosphere you perceived during the shoot, it is due to the fact that you filled your picture with lots of unexpected and undesired elements which created distractions in the picture. Rather than just aimlessly point your camera at wide areas, try to discover the most spectacular aspect of the scenery and enhance it using telephotos settings. In the picture above, areas with impressive autumn foliage were boldly focused on.

Focal lengths: 150mm, f-stops: 11.0, Shutter speeds: 1/4second.

Telephotos shooting are likewise good for displaying pictures with compressed depths of sceneries. Though all the elements in this picture – mountains, conifer trees and yellow trees – are several kilometers apart, they're tightly compressed to create a spectacular picture.

Create expressions using different ideas and viewpoints

Autumn shoots are not restricted to shooting just leaves and trees. You could incorporate lakes, streams, mountains, as well as other objects in the environment to enhance the beauty of autumn foliage; fallen leaves likewise creates expressions of autumn landscapes. You could try shooting different compositions of different subjects from broad perspectives and bask in the liberty of shooting pictures of autumn foliage.

(1) Focal lengths: 50mm, f-stops: 2.8, Shutter speeds: 1/8second.

(2) Focal lengths: 70mm, f-stops: 7.1, Shutter speeds: 1/160second.

(1) Pictures of fallen leaves drifting across the surface of puddles close to your foot indicates that autumn is at an end. Autumn foliage isn't restricted to trees adorned with crimson red. There are traces of autumn everywhere even after the colors of autumn

leaves.

(2) Even droplets of water on a fallen leaf evokes an atmosphere of autumn.

Focal lengths: 35mm, f-stops: 10.0, Shutter speeds: 1/15second.

Rivers, ponds, and lakes which often play second fiddle to autumn trees and foliage are the major actors at times. Also note the reflection of colorful trees across the surfaces of water bodies.

Trying wide-angled lenses

F-number: 8/Shutter speeds: 1/100sec.

SEL1635Z

This full-framed E-mounts 16 to 35mm ZEISS Vario-Tessar zooms offer impressive performance with its compact, lightweight design. Its multipurpose zoom range alongside its inbuilt optical images stabilizations makes it the perfect lens for shooting landscapes, group shots, indoor scenes, snapshots, and lots more, particularly with its full-framed α7 series build. Its constant maximum aperture of F4 facilitates the control of depth-of-field and exposure.

Capturing Beautiful Illuminations

Whenever the beautiful illuminations of cityscapes are in view, chances are that you'll like to shoot them. We will show you exactly how to shoot illuminations such that the picture traps the atmosphere present at the scene. During the shoot, set your camera to A-modes to enable you personalize aperture. In general, to be able to focus on the whole scene, you must reduce aperture, and increase it to the fullest to lay emphasis on an aspect and shoot closeup shots of decorations or illuminations.

Photographing the Whole Scene

When shooting illuminations, at times, you might decide to shoot entire scenes as cityscapes and at other times, you might decide to shoot closeups of your subjects.

Entire scenes captured. Focal lengths: 24mm (35mm equiv.), f-stops: 2.8, Shutter speeds: 1/60second.

Close-ups captured. Focal lengths: 50mm, f-stops: 1.8, Shutter speeds: 1/80second.

Generally, when capturing entire scenes, you could try setting Creative Look/Creative Style, white balance, and exposure compensations to similar settings like when taking night shots.

Aperture setting

To focus your camera on entire scenes, shoot with smaller apertures. You can shoot beautiful pictures with entire scenes in focus when you set aperture values within the ranges of f8 and 11. However, if you're not using tripods, you must prioritize the prevention of camera shake. Even while shooting entire scenes, open aperture extremely wide.

Exposure compensation

The basic rule for shooting illuminations is to alter brightness to produce the overall feel. Adjusting exposure compensation towards + results in very vibrant pictures, based on the settings of your camera and the source of light.

Exposure compensations: 0 (when set at multi-patterns metering).

Exposure compensations: +1.3 (when set at multi-patterns metering).

Since illumination lightings deals with increased differences between dark and bright regions compared to shooting regular night scenes, there might be higher contrasts and you might be unable to shoot the scene before you just by adjusting exposure compensation. When this happens, try to adjust DRO (D-Range Optimizers).

DRO analyses images and obtains optimal brightness for every area within the picture. As against exposure compensations that evenly decreases or increases the general brightness of images, this function only adjusts brightness in overexposed and underexposed regions, which is particularly handy whenever there are extreme light contrasts.

When shooting illuminations, you can only see the impact of this function at Levels 3 to 5 (stronger levels). However, when you overdo the correction, it could result in noticeable noise and unnatural pictures, so choose optimal levels by observing the pictures you have already shot.

DRO: Off.

DRO: Lv5.

In the above instance, DRO was fixed at Lv5. With DRO activated, darker regions are brightened resulting in a picture closer in appearance to how the scene is viewed with the human eye. Auto HDR is another handy function which simultaneously captures three pictures using different exposures, and afterwards overlaps the pictures to portray both the dark and bright areas. Check the Handbook or User Manual for details on using Auto HDR and DRO.

White balance

When you change white balance, it becomes possible to change the expressions of illuminated pictures. Though Auto WB faithfully reproduces colors to how they are perceived with the human eye, using Daylight, you can likewise create warm images or using Incandescent to produce ethereal or cold images.

White-balance: AWB.

White-balance: Sunlight.

White-balance: Incandescent.

Creative Style/Creative Look

When adjusting exposure compensations, white balance and DRO won't suffice, you could additionally adjust saturation under Creative Look/Creative Style towards +. This causes the illumination lightings to appear more impressive. We also advise changing the settings under Creative Look/Creative Style. Experiment with the numerous settings on Creative Look/Creative Style.

Creative Styles: Standard, no saturations adjustment.

Creative Styles: Standard, saturations adjusted towards +

Shooting Close-ups

When capturing illumination lightings, try shooting closeups of surrounding small objects and decorations. Closeups of only illumination lightings tend to enhance the wires and light bulbs, hence focusing on close-by decorations or getting the right angle of the background could result in spectacular images.

(1) Captured at eye level.

(2) Captured from another angle.

Here's a closeup shot of Christmas tree ornaments. Picture (1) was captured just focusing on the ornaments without altering the background. Since there aren't any illuminations on its background, the whole picture appears dark, and has a poor balance. In picture (2), camera angles were set to capture the background tree.

This picture has improved balance compared to picture (1), and gorgeously communicates the beautiful surroundings. You could further defocus its background by opening aperture very wide, however with auto exposures, the picture looked dark, and as a result, exposures compensation was adjusted towards +. The above image at the right is an alternative picture of small primary subjects under focus while illumination becomes secondary subjects in the compositions.

Defocusing illuminations in the foregrounds. Focal lengths: 70mm (35mm equiv.), f-stops: 2.8, Shutter speeds: 1/100second.

Shots can be taken to defocus illuminations in foregrounds just like with backgrounds. Creating large circular blurs of illuminations can make images appear magical. The number and size of round blurs varies greatly, based on the angle of the camera, your distance from the light, and the illumination. To get optimal photo balance, capture several images while in motion. If you're unable to focus on subjects in backgrounds, use MF (manual focus).

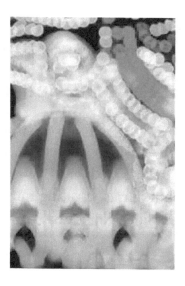

(1) Focal lengths: 130mm, f-stops: 5.6, Shutter speeds: 1/200second.

(2) Focal lengths: 91mm, f-stops: 5.6, Shutter speeds: 1/125second,
using cross filters.

For picture (1), focus was adjusted using manual focus causing everything to appear blurred. With this, you can capture interesting images when subjects are only illumination lightings.

Also, depending on the application, you can use a commercially available cross filter to create a brilliant image, as shown in (2).

Using Fixed Focal Lengths Lenses

With Fixed Focal Lengths Lenses, you can shoot impressive pictures with backgrounds increasingly defocused, which is handy for photographing illuminations. Fixed Focal Lengths Lenses trap more light compared to zoom lenses, creating minimal blur for a more convenient shoot even under dim areas.

Focal lengths: 55mm/F-numbers: 2.2/Shutter speed: 1/15sec.

This is a standard prime lens comprising 55mm focal lengths and large maximum apertures of F1.8. It offers impressive ZEISS Sonnar resolution and contrasts for full-framed E-mounts bodies. It additionally creates gorgeous backgrounds bokeh for setting off subjects when the need arises. The big, vibrant maximum aperture implies that you can capture handheld under low-light environments while still achieving impressive clarity and sharpness.

f-stops: 1.8, Shutter speeds: 1/80second.

SEL50F18

This is a medium telephotos lens with focal lengths of 75mm (35mm equiv.), handy for shooting portraits. Bright apertures of f1.8 as well as its new optics systems enable you capture gorgeous blurred pictures. When you combine this with optical images stabilization's function, this lens proves its efficacy in handheld photography even under darker conditions.

Additionally, the internal focusing and inbuilt motor provides silent and smooth AF, good for recording movies. The lens comprises aluminum alloys exteriors for high-quality appearances.

FOCUS SETTING

When capturing standard moving subjects with the Alpha 9, the below settings are suggested by default.

Install the most recent version of the system software on the camera.

Recommended default settings

Focus Mode	AF-C	Focus mode dial
Focus Area *	Flexible Spot: M	[📷1 (Camera Settings1)] 4 / 13 (AF1)
Face/Eye AF Set. *	Face/Eye Priority in AF: [On]	[📷1 (Camera Settings1)] 5 / 13 (AF2)
Priority Set in AF-C	Balanced Emphasis	[📷1 (Camera Settings1)] 4 / 13 (AF1)
AF Track Sens *	3(Standard)	[📷1 (Camera Settings1)] 5 / 13 (AF2)
Swt. V/H AF Area	AF Point Only	[📷1 (Camera Settings1)] 4 / 13 (AF1)

Suggested settings differ based on your subject. Take a look at the chart below.

The Focus Mode: Continuous AF

When configured to the Continuous AF (AF-C) mode, your camera will continue to focus as your shutter key is being pressed & held midway through (down).

The Focus Area: The Flexible Spots M

If configured to your Flexible Spot ⊞, your camera lets you move your focusing frame into your desired point in your lens & focus on small subject on a narrow zone. Your focusing frame's size can be chosen. For general utilization, it is suggested to use the average size M. Take a look at the chart below for every subject setting.

Additional settings

- ⊡ **The Wide:** Focuses automatically on subject across your whole screen.
- ⊡ **The Zone:** Once the individual chooses its focus zone in the screen, the camera therefore will auto choose its focus points.
- ⊡ **The Center:** This focuses auto on the object in the middle of the picture.
- ⊞ **The Expand Flexible Spots:** When the camera can't focus in one chosen point, then it flexibly utilizes focus points over that spot as supplementary region for focusing.
- ⊡, ⊡, ⊡, ⊞, ⊞ **Tracking :** Pressing and holding your shutter button midway allows the device to track the object inside the designated autofocus area. If your focus mode has been configured to (AF-C), only then is this setting accessible.

  On your (Focus Area) setup screen, point the pointer to (Tracking). Then, utilizing the right and left control wheel, choose the area you want to initiate tracking in. setting up the regions as an expand flexible spots, flexible spot, or zone will allow you to relocate the monitoring start zone to the required location.

System software Version. 5.00 or advance

Eye/Face Autofocus Setting

Eye/Fac Priority on Autofocus: Turn (On)

The purpose of this option is to select whether your camera will prioritize focusing on human eyes or faces. When autofocus is engaged, the camera finds a subject's face inside the focus area and focuses on that subject's eyes or face. Additionally, if (Focus Area) has been configured to (Tracking)j, the camera automatically focus in the eyes or face as soon as it detects a face close to its focusing frame while tracking. If the object is an individual, this function works well.

Priority Set in Continuous AF: Balanced Emphasis

When deciding whether to press the shutter release even when the object is out of focus, captures with balanced emphasis is both shutter release and focusing.

Auto Focus – Subject-track Sensitivity: three (Standard)

- If configured to five (Responsive), your camera focuses quickly on objects at separate distances.

- If configured to one (Locked on), your camera places your focus in a certain individual even if a different object passes the subject's front.
- Standard three is suggested for general utilization. Take a look at the chart below for every subject's setting.

Switch Vertical/Horizontal Auto focus area: only AF Point

- Changes the focusing frame's location based on the camera's orientation (vertical or horizontal). The (Focusing Region) is fixed.

Additional settings

- **Off**: Doesn't switch the (Focusing Region) or the location of your focusing frame depending on the camera's orientation (vertical or horizontal).
- **Autofocus Area + Autofocus Point:** Changes both the (Focusing Region) and the focusing frame's location on the camera's orientation (vertical or horizontal).

Suggested AF settings chart for all subject

Ball games

Subject	Focus Mode	Focus Area	Face/Eye AF Set.	Other settings
Soccer, Football, Futsal	AF-C	[Flexible Spot: M] [Expand Flexible Spot]	Face/Eye Priority in AF: [On] Subject Detection: [Human]	Priority Set in AF-C: [Balanced Emphasis] AF Tracking Sens.: [4] Switch V/H AF Area (still image): [AF Point Only]
Basketball	AF-C	[Flexible Spot: M] [Expand Flexible Spot]	Face/Eye Priority in AF: [On] Subject Detection: [Human]	Priority Set in AF-C: [Balanced Emphasis] AF Tracking Sens.: [3 (Standard)] Switch V/H AF Area (still image): [AF Point Only]
Rugby	AF-C	[Flexible Spot: M] [Expand Flexible Spot]	Face/Eye Priority in AF: [On] Subject Detection: [Human]	Priority Set in AF-C: [Balanced Emphasis] AF Tracking Sens.: [3 (Standard)] Switch V/H AF Area

American football	AF-C	[Flexible Spot: M] [Expand Flexible Spot]	Face/Eye Priority in AF: [Off]	Priority Set in AF-C: [Balanced Emphasis] AF Tracking Sens.: [2] Switch V/H AF Area (still image): [AF Point Only]
Handball	AF-C	[Flexible Spot: M] [Expand Flexible Spot]	Face/Eye Priority in AF: [On] Subject Detection: [Human]	Priority Set in AF-C: [Balanced Emphasis] AF Tracking Sens.: [4] Switch V/H AF Area (still image): [AF Point Only]
Tennis	AF-C	[Flexible Spot: M] [Expand Flexible Spot] [Tracking:	Face/Eye Priority in AF: [On] Subject Detection: [Human]	Priority Set in AF-C: [Balanced Emphasis] AF Tracking Sens.: [3 (Standard)] Switch V/H AF Area
Volleyball	AF-C	[Flexible Spot: M] [Expand Flexible Spot]	Face/Eye Priority in AF: [On] Subject Detection: [Human]	Priority Set in AF-C: [Balanced Emphasis] AF Tracking Sens.: [3 (Standard)] Switch V/H AF Area (still image): [AF Point Only]
Sepak takraw	AF-C	[Flexible Spot: M] [Expand Flexible Spot] [Zone]	Face/Eye Priority in AF: [Off]	Priority Set in AF-C: [Balanced Emphasis] AF Tracking Sens.: [3 (Standard)] Switch V/H AF Area (still image): [AF Point Only]

Subject	Focus Mode	Focus Area	Face/Eye AF Set.	Other settings
Sprints (100 m~), Hurdles	AF-C	[Flexible Spot: M] [Expand Flexible Spot] [Tracking: Flexible Spot M]	Face/Eye Priority in AF: [On] Subject Detection: [Human]	Priority Set in AF-C: [Balanced Emphasis] AF Tracking Sens.: [3 (Standard)] Switch V/H AF Area (still image): [AF Point Only]
Javelin, Shot put	AF-C	[Flexible Spot: M] [Expand Flexible Spot] [Tracking:	Face/Eye Priority in AF: [On] Subject Detection: [Human]	Priority Set in AF-C: [Balanced Emphasis] AF Tracking Sens.: [3

215

		Flexible Spot M]		(Standard)] Switch V/H AF Area (still image): [AF Point Only]
Long jump, Triple jump	AF-C	[Flexible Spot: M] [Expand Flexible Spot] [Tracking: Flexible Spot M]	Face/Eye Priority in AF: [On] Subject Detection: [Human]	Priority Set in AF-C: [Balanced Emphasis] AF Tracking Sens.: [3 (Standard)] Switch V/H AF Area (still image): [AF Point Only]
High jump, Pole vault	AF-C	[Flexible Spot: M] [Expand Flexible Spot]	Face/Eye Priority in AF: [Off]	Priority Set in AF-C: [Balanced Emphasis] AF Tracking
Marathon	AF-C	[Flexible Spot: M] [Expand Flexible Spot] [Tracking: Flexible Spot M]	Face/Eye Priority in AF: [On] Subject Detection: [Human]	Priority Set in AF-C: [Balanced Emphasis] AF Tracking Sens.: [3 (Standard)] Switch V/H AF Area (still image): [AF Point Only]

Winter sports

Subject	Focus Mode	Focus Area	Face/Eye AF Set.	Other settings
Alpine skiing (near a gate, jump)	AF-C	[Flexible Spot: M] [Expand Flexible Spot] [Tracking: Flexible Spot M]	Face/Eye Priority in AF: [On] Subject Detection: [Human]	Priority Set in AF-C: [Balanced Emphasis] AF Tracking Sens.: [3 (Standard)] Switch V/H AF Area (still image): [AF Point Only]
Mogul	AF-C	[Flexible Spot: M] [Expand Flexible Spot] [Tracking: Flexible Spot M]	Face/Eye Priority in AF: [On] Subject Detection: [Human]	Priority Set in AF-C: [Balanced Emphasis] AF Tracking Sens.: [3 (Standard)] Switch V/H AF Area (still image):

				[AF Point Only]
Snowboarding (Halfpipe, Slalom)	AF-C	[Flexible Spot: M] [Expand Flexible Spot] [Tracking: Flexible Spot M]	Face/Eye Priority in AF: [On] Subject Detection: [Human]	Priority Set in AF-C: [Balanced Emphasis] AF Tracking Sens.: [3 (Standard)] Switch V/H AF Area (still image): [AF Point Only]
Ski jumping (front, side)	AF-C	[Flexible Spot: M] [Expand Flexible Spot] [Tracking: Flexible Spot M]	Face/Eye Priority in AF: [On] Subject Detection: [Human]	Priority Set in AF-C: [Balanced Emphasis] AF Tracking Sens.: [3 (Standard)] Switch V/H AF Area (still image): [AF Point Only]

Biathlon	AF-C	[Flexible Spot: M] [Expand Flexible Spot] [Tracking: Flexible Spot M]	Face/Eye Priority in AF: [On] Subject Detection: [Human]	Priority Set in AF-C: [Balanced Emphasis] AF Tracking Sens.: [3 (Standard)] Switch V/H AF Area (still image): [AF Point Only]
Short-track speed skating	AF-C	[Flexible Spot: M] [Expand Flexible Spot] [Tracking: Flexible Spot M]	Face/Eye Priority in AF: [On] Subject Detection: [Human]	Priority Set in AF-C: [Balanced Emphasis] AF Tracking Sens.: [3 (Standard)] Switch V/H AF Area (still image): [AF Point Only]
Speed skating	AF-C	[Flexible Spot: M]	Face/Eye Priority in	Priority Set in AF-C:

		[Zone] [Tracking: Flexible Spot M]	AF: [On] Subject Detection: [Human]	[Balanced Emphasis] AF Tracking Sens.: [3 (Standard)] Switch V/H AF Area (still image): [AF Point Only]
Figure skating (Singles)	AF-C	[Tracking: Flexible Spot M] [Flexible Spot: M] [Zone]	Face/Eye Priority in AF: [On] Subject Detection: [Human]	Priority Set in AF-C: [Balanced Emphasis] AF Tracking Sens.: [3 (Standard)] Switch V/H AF Area (still image): [AF Point Only]
Ice hockey	AF-C	[Flexible Spot: M] [Expand	Face/Eye Priority in AF: [Off]	Priority Set in AF-C: [Balanced Emphasis]

		Flexible Spot]		AF Tracking Sens.: [4] Switch V/H AF Area (still image): [AF Point Only]
Curling	AF-C	[Tracking: Flexible Spot M] [Flexible Spot: M] [Expand Flexible Spot]	Face/Eye Priority in AF: [On] Subject Detection: [Human]	Priority Set in AF-C: [Balanced Emphasis] AF Tracking Sens.: [2] Switch V/H AF Area (still image): [AF Point Only]
Bobsleigh	AF-C	[Flexible Spot: M] [Expand Flexible Spot] [Tracking: Flexible Spot M]	Face/Eye Priority in AF: [On] Subject Detection: [Human]	Priority Set in AF-C: [Balanced Emphasis] AF Tracking Sens.: [3 (Standard)] Switch V/H
				AF Area (still image): [AF Point Only]

221

Motor sports

Subject	Focus Mode	Focus Area	Face/Eye AF Set.	Other settings
Car racing, Karting	AF-C	[Flexible Spot: M] [Expand Flexible Spot] [Tracking: Flexible Spot M]	Face/Eye Priority in AF: [Off]	Priority Set in AF-C: [Balanced Emphasis] AF Tracking Sens.: [3 (Standard)] Switch V/H AF Area (still image): [AF Point Only]
Motorcycling (on-road)	AF-C	[Flexible Spot: M] [Expand Flexible Spot] [Tracking: Flexible Spot M]	Face/Eye Priority in AF: [Off]	Priority Set in AF-C: [Balanced Emphasis] AF Tracking Sens.: [3 (Standard)] Switch V/H AF Area (still image): [AF Point Only]
Motocross	AF-C	[Flexible Spot: M] [Wide] [Tracking: Wide]	Face/Eye Priority in AF: [Off]	Priority Set in AF-C: [Balanced Emphasis] AF Tracking Sens.: [3 (Standard)] Switch V/H AF Area (still image): [AF Point Only]

Subject	Focus Mode	Focus Area	Face/Eye AF Set.	Other settings
		[Flexible Spot: M]	Subject Detection: [Human]	Emphasis] AF Tracking Sens.: [1(Locked on)] to [2] Switch V/H AF Area (still image): [AF Point Only]
Cycle race	AF-C	[Flexible Spot: M] [Expand Flexible Spot] [Tracking: Flexible Spot M]	Face/Eye Priority in AF: [On] Subject Detection: [Human]	Priority Set in AF-C: [Balanced Emphasis] AF Tracking Sens.: [3 (Standard)] Switch V/H AF Area (still image): [AF Point Only]

Other sports

Subject	Focus Mode	Focus Area	Face/Eye AF Set.	Other settings
Archery	AF-C	[Tracking: Flexible Spot M] [Flexible Spot: M] [Expand Flexible Spot]	Face/Eye Priority in AF: [On] Subject Detection: [Human]	Priority Set in AF-C: [Balanced Emphasis] AF Tracking Sens.: [3 (Standard)] Switch V/H AF Area (still image): [AF Point Only]
Canoeing, Equestrian events	AF-C	[Flexible Spot: M] [Expand Flexible Spot] [Tracking: Flexible Spot M]	Face/Eye Priority in AF: [On] Subject Detection: [Human]	Priority Set in AF-C: [Balanced Emphasis] AF Tracking Sens.: [2] Switch V/H AF Area (still image): [AF Point Only]

Subject	Focus Mode	Focus Area	Face/Eye AF Set.	Other settings
Judo	AF-C	[Flexible Spot: M] [Expand Flexible Spot]	Face/Eye Priority in AF: [On] Subject Detection: [Human]	Priority Set in AF-C: [Balanced Emphasis] AF Tracking Sens.: [3 (Standard)] Switch V/H AF Area (still image): [AF Point Only]
Kendo	AF-C	[Flexible Spot: M] [Expand Flexible Spot]	Face/Eye Priority in AF: [Off]	Priority Set in AF-C: [Balanced Emphasis] AF Tracking Sens.: [3 (Standard)] Switch V/H AF Area (still image): [AF Point Only]

Subject	Focus Mode	Focus Area	Face/Eye AF Set.	Other settings
Horseracing	AF-C	[Tracking: Flexible Spot M] [Flexible Spot: M] [Expand Flexible Spot]	Face/Eye Priority in AF: [On] Subject Detection: [Human]	Priority Set in AF-C: [Balanced Emphasis] AF Tracking Sens.: [3 (Standard)] Switch V/H AF Area (still image): [AF Point Only]
Equestrian events	AF-C	[Flexible Spot: M] [Expand Flexible Spot] [Tracking: Flexible Spot M]	Face/Eye Priority in AF: [On] Subject Detection: [Human]	Priority Set in AF-C: [Balanced Emphasis] AF Tracking Sens.: [2] Switch V/H AF Area (still image): [AF Point Only]

Other sports

Subject	Focus Mode	Focus Area	Face/Eye AF Set.	Other settings
Speedboat racing	AF-C	[Tracking: Flexible Spot M] [Flexible Spot: M] [Expand Flexible Spot]	Face/Eye Priority in AF: [Off]	Priority Set in AF-C: [Balanced Emphasis] AF Tracking Sens.: [3 (Standard)] Switch V/H AF Area (still image): [AF Point Only]
Fencing	AF-C	[Flexible Spot: M] [Expand Flexible Spot] [Tracking: Flexible Spot M]	Face/Eye Priority in AF: [Off]	Priority Set in AF-C: [Balanced Emphasis] AF Tracking Sens.: [3 (Standard)] Switch V/H AF Area (still image): [AF Point Only]

Subject	Focus Mode	Focus Area	Face/Eye AF Set.	Other settings
Gymnastics, rhythmic gymnastics	AF-C	[Tracking: Flexible Spot M] [Flexible Spot: M] [Expand Flexible Spot]	Face/Eye Priority in AF: [On] Subject Detection: [Human]	Priority Set in AF-C: [Balanced Emphasis] AF Tracking Sens.: [3 (Standard)] Switch V/H AF Area (still image): [AF Point Only]
Golf	AF-C	[Tracking: Flexible Spot M] [Flexible Spot: M] [Expand Flexible Spot]	Face/Eye Priority in AF: [On] Subject Detection: [Human]	Priority Set in AF-C: [Balanced Emphasis] AF Tracking Sens.: [2] Switch V/H AF Area (still image): [AF Point Only]

Other sports

Subject	Focus Mode	Focus Area	Face/Eye AF Set.	Other settings

Non-sport categories

Subject	Focus Mode	Focus Area	Face/Eye AF Set.	Other settings
Trains and other railed vehicles	AF-C	[Tracking: Flexible Spot M] [Flexible Spot: M] [Expand Flexible Spot]	Face/Eye Priority in AF: [Off]	Priority Set in AF-C: [Balanced Emphasis] AF Tracking Sens.: [3 (Standard)] Switch V/H AF Area (still image): [AF Point Only]
Airplanes, Air shows	AF-C	[Tracking: Flexible Spot M] [Flexible Spot: M] [Zone]	Face/Eye Priority in AF: [Off]	Priority Set in AF-C: [Balanced Emphasis] AF Tracking Sens.: [3 (Standard)] Switch V/H AF Area (still image): [AF Point Only]

Subject	Focus Mode	Focus Area	Face/Eye AF Set.	Other settings
Wild birds	AF-C	[Flexible Spot: M] [Expand Flexible Spot] [Tracking: Wide]	Face/Eye Priority in AF: [Off]	Priority Set in AF-C: [Balanced Emphasis] AF Tracking Sens.: [3 (Standard)] Switch V/H AF Area (still image): [AF Point Only]
Wild animals	AF-C	[Flexible Spot: M] [Expand Flexible Spot] [Tracking: Flexible Spot M]	Face/Eye Priority in AF: [On] Subject Detection: [Animal]	Priority Set in AF-C: [Balanced Emphasis] AF Tracking Sens.: [2] Switch V/H AF Area (still image): [AF Point Only]

For each sport, below are a few shooting guides and recommended settings, focusing on variations from the suggested default settings.

- Install the most recent version of the system software on the camera.

Subjects and Events

Handball, Futsal, Football, Soccer

Recommended settings

Focus Area	[Flexible Spot: M] [Expand Flexible Spot]
Face/Eye AF Set.	Face/Eye Priority in AF: [On] Subject Detection: [Human]
Priority Set in AF-C	[Balanced Emphasis]
AF Track Sens	[4]
Swt. V/H AF Area	[AF Point Only]

Set Autofocus subject-track sensitivity into the reasonably responsive lvl four to handle repeated passes as well as players crossing on the subject's front.

- If you are photographing many subjects near together or a subject that is more distant, configure the focus area to [Expand Flex Spot] instead of [Flex Spot: M].

Volleyball, Basketball

Recommended settings

Focus Area	[Flexible Spot: M] [Expand Flexible Spot]
Face/Eye AF Set.	Face/Eye Priority in AF: [On] Subject Detection: [Human]
Priority Set in AF-C	[Balanced Emphasis]
AF Track Sens	[3 (Standard)]
Swt. V/H AF Area	[AF Point Only]

Autofocus subjects-track sensitivity three (Standard) is suggested for steady tracking if other players repeatedly cross in the subject's front. [Flex Spot: M], is the most useful focus area setting, is suggested. If the subject that you wish to shoot may be framed inside the configuration, [Expand Flex Spot] may be utilized for more chosen focus.

Tennis

Recommended settings

Focus Area	[Flexible Spot: M] [Expand Flexible Spot] [Tracking: Flexible Spot M]
Face/Eye AF Set.	Face/Eye Priority in AF: [On] Subject Detection: [Human]
Priority Set in AF-C	[Balanced Emphasis]
AF Track Sens	[3 (Standard)]
Swt. V/H AF Area	[AF Point Only]

- **[Expand Flex Spot]/[Flex Spot: M]**

Autofocus subjects-track sensitivity three (Standard) is suggested for steady tracking if other players repeatedly cross in the subject's front. [Flex Spot: M], is the most useful focus area setting, is suggested. If the subject that you wish to shoot may be framed inside the configuration, [Expand Flex Spot] may be utilized for more chosen focus.

- **Tracking: [Flex Spot M]**

You should configure the focus area to [Tracking: Flex Spot M] while capturing moderate details of tennis competitors in singles play or other scenarios with fast horizontal movement. If you adjust [Eye/Face Priority on Autofocus] to [ON] as well as utilize it in conjunction with your tracking function, your camera automatically track eyes and faces if the individual's body is within the focus area and the face detection becomes available.

You can adjust the framing while following the subject to suit your tastes. This makes compositional changes possible, including balancing the background and other subjects in the shot.

The camera might be unable to choose the desired focus point when the tracking function is ON if it detects faces besides the subjects, like audience member's or a referee's, close to the focus area. It is advised that you configure [Eye/Face Priority on Autofocus] to [OFF] when the focus area shifts towards a face besides your subject's.

Utilizing [Flex Spot: M]. Alternatively, tapping the shutter key midway through again is beneficial when rapidly capturing several subjects in sequence.

Assigning [Reg. Custom Shoots Set] or [Tracking On] (Set to Autofocus Tracking and On) into the Custom Button enables you to swiftly change your tracking function off or on.

Rugby

Recommended settings

Focus Area	[Expand Flexible Spot] [Flexible Spot: M]
Face/Eye AF Set.	Face/Eye Priority in AF: [On] Subject Detection: [Human]
Priority Set in AF-C	[Balanced Emphasis]
AF Track Sens	[3 (Standard)]
Swt. V/H AF Area	[AF Point Only]

Autofocus subjects-track sensitivity three (Standard) is suggested for steady tracking if other players repeatedly cross in the subject's front. Configuring the focus area to [Expand Flex Spot], is suggested more chosen focus in the subject, especially when focusing in a particular subject on a crowd to other subjects.

American football

Recommended settings

Focus Area	[Expand Flexible Spot] [Flexible Spot: M]
Face/Eye AF Set.	Face/Eye Priority in AF: [Off]
Priority Set in AF-C	[Balanced Emphasis]
AF Track Sens	[2]
Swt. V/H AF Area	[AF Point Only]

Where the players are both crossing and crashing with one another, configure Autofocus subject-tracking awareness to two to track a player steadily and repeatedly. As the players are always crowded with each other in this game, [Expand Flex Spot] becomes suggested while focusing on one subject on a group to several other subjects.

The Sepak takraw

Recommended settings

Focus Area	[Flexible Spot: M] [Expand Flexible Spot] [Zone]
Face/Eye AF Set.	Face/Eye Priority in AF: [Off]
Priority Set in AF-C	[Balanced Emphasis]
AF Track Sens	[3 (Standard)]
Swt. V/H AF Area	[AF Point Only]

Effectiveness can be achieved with the flexible default recommended settings (focus area: [Flex Spot: M]; Autofocus subject-tracking awareness: Standard three). Try adjusting the responsiveness to a stronger two and your focus area into [Expand Flex Spot] when there are several barriers.

To make it easier to focus on the subjects moving quickly, change your focus area into [Zone] when the individual is advancing too quickly for you to use [Flex Spot: M]. Face detection can be challenging on sports where the individual's faces are hidden. It is advised that you adjust [Eye/Face Priority in Autofocus] into [Off] when your focus area shifts towards a face besides your subject's

Pole vault, High jump

Recommended settings

Focus Area	[Flexible Spot: M] [Expand Flexible Spot]
Face/Eye AF Set.	Face/Eye Priority in AF: [Off]
Priority Set in AF-C	[Balanced Emphasis]
AF Track Sens	[3 (Standard)]
Swt. V/H AF Area	[AF Point Only]

Configuring the Autofocus subject-tracking awareness to three (Standard) increases tracking stability, with your focus more likely to move to the subject's hand or a pole. Configuring your focus area into [Flex Spot: M], also becomes suggested for a much steadier focus. When the focus area shifts into a face besides your individual's, it is suggested that you configure [Eye/Face Priority in Autofocus] to [Off].

Field and track events (Track and field events (not including the pole jump and high jump)

Recommended settings

Focus Area	[Flexible Spot: M] [Expand Flexible Spot] [Tracking: Flexible Spot M]
Face/Eye AF Set.	Face/Eye Priority in AF: [On] Subject Detection: [Human]
Priority Set in AF-C	[Balanced Emphasis]
AF Track Sens	[3 (Standard)]
Swt. V/H AF Area	[AF Point Only]

- **[Expand Flex Spot]/[Flex Spot: M]**

For much steadier focus on scenarios where objects move in the subject's front in which you wish to focus, suggested setting is [Expand Flex Spot]/[Flex Spot: M].

Setting the Autofocus subject-tracking awareness much steadier, with your focus less probable to move subject's hand or a pole.

- **[Tracking: Flex Spot: M]**

Adjusting your focus are into [Tracking: Flex Spot M] was suggested for repeatedly tracking one subject.

When you configure [Eye/Face Priority in Autofocus] into [On] and utilize it in conjunction with your tracking function, your camera automatically track eyes and faces when the individual's body is within the focus area and the face detection becomes available. Tracking the individual, the framing may be changed based on your preference. It allows for modifications to the arrangement, like balancing backgrounds and other subjects inside the shot.

The face detection can be challenging in events in which the individual's faces are obscured, like your shot put. When your focus area shifts into a face besides your subject's, therefore, it is suggested that you configure [Eye/Face Priority in Autofocus] to [Off].

Holding your shutter button midway or utilizing Flexible Spot again is useful while quickly shooting several subjects in sequence. Assigning [Reg. Custom Shoots Set] or [Tracking On] (Set to Autofocus Tracking and On) into the Custom button enables you to rapidly change your tracking function off or on.

Short-track speeds skating, Bobsleigh, Biathlon, Ski jumping, Snowboarding, Mogul, Skiing

Recommended settings

Focus Area	[Flexible Spot: M] [Expand Flexible Spot] [Tracking: Flexible Spot M]
Face/Eye AF Set.	Face/Eye Priority in AF: [On] Subject Detection: [Human]
Priority Set in AF-C	[Balanced Emphasis]
AF Track Sens	[3 (Standard)]
Swt. V/H AF Area	[AF Point Only]

- **[Expand Flex Spot]/[Flex Spot: M]**

Configure Autofocus subjects-track sensitivity to three (Standard) for steady tracking of your subject on alpine skiing in which athletes pass in front of poles, or the short-track speeds skating in which the leader alternates regularly.

The suggested setting for your focus area is the adaptable [Flex Spot: M], nevertheless, when the subject is farther away or when different players are near each other like in the short-track speeds skating, [Expand Flex Spot] is suggested.

- **[Tracking: Flex Spot M]**

Adjusting your focus area into [Tracking: Flex Spot M] was suggested for repeatedly tracking one subject. When you configure [Eye/Face Priority in Autofocus] into [On] and utilize it in conjunction with your tracking function, your camera automatically track eyes and faces when the individual's body is within the focus area and the face detection becomes available.

Tracking the individual, the framing may be changed based on your preference. It allows for modifications to the arrangement, like balancing backgrounds and other subjects inside the shot.

Assigning [Reg. Custom Shoots Set] or [Tracking On] (Set to Autofocus Tracking and On) into the Custom button enables you to rapidly change your tracking function off or on.

The face detection can be challenging in events, like when an individual is wearing big goggles.

When your focus area shifts into a face besides your subject's, therefore, it is suggested that you configure [Eye/Face Priority in Autofocus] to [Off].

The Speed skating

Recommended settings

Focus Area	[Flexible Spot: M] [Zone] [Tracking: Flexible Spot M]
Face/Eye AF Set.	Face/Eye Priority in AF: [On] Subject Detection: [Human]
Priority Set in AF-C	[Balanced Emphasis]
AF Track Sens	[3 (Standard)]
Swt. V/H AF Area	[AF Point Only]

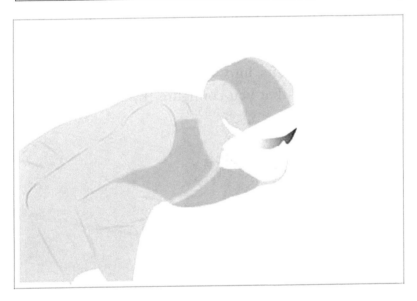

- **[Zone]/[Flex Spot: M]**

For much steadier focus on scenarios where objects move in the subject's front in which you wish to focus, suggested setting is [Zone] or [Flex Spot: M].

When the individual is moving rapidly to focus using [Flex Spot: M], configure your focus area into [Zone] to much easier focus on individuals moving at greater speed.

- **[Tracking: Flexible Spot M]**

Configuring your focus area into [Tracking: Flex Spot M] was suggested for repeatedly tracking one subject.

Focusing repeatedly on a particular individual, it is suggested that you configure [Eye/Face Priority in Autofocus] into [On] and utilize it in conjunction with your tracking function. Your camera automatically track eyes and faces when the individual's body is within the focus area and the face detection becomes available.

Tracking the individual, the framing may be changed based on your preference. It allows for modifications to the arrangement, like balancing backgrounds and other subjects inside the shot.

When the individual is moving very fast to coincide your focus area, choose [Tracking: Zone] so you can shoot the individual more readily.

The Figure skater (Singles)

Recommended settings

Focus Area	[Tracking: Flexible Spot M] [Flexible Spot: M] [Zone]
Face/Eye AF Set.	Face/Eye Priority in AF: [On] Subject Detection: [Human]
Priority Set in AF-C	[Balanced Emphasis]
AF Track Sens	[3 (Standard)]
Swt. V/H AF Area	[AF Point Only]

- [Tracking: Flex Spot M]

While taking a solo capture of a particular figure skater while on a show (singles), it's therefore, advised that you configure your focus area into [Tracking: Flex Spot M].

Focusing repeatedly on a particular individual, it is suggested that you configure [Eye/Face Priority in Autofocus] into [On] and utilize it in conjunction with your tracking function.

Your camera automatically track eyes and faces when the individual's body is within the focus area and the face detection becomes available. Tracking the individual, the framing may be changed based on your preference. It allows for modifications to the arrangement, like balancing backgrounds and other subjects inside the shot.

Assigning [Reg. Custom Shoots Set] or [Tracking On] (Set to Autofocus Tracking and On) into the Custom button enables you to rapidly change your tracking function off or on.

- **[Zone]/[Flex Spot: M]**

For much steadier focus on scenarios where objects move in the subject's front in which you wish to focus, suggested setting is [Zone] or [Flex Spot: M].

When the individual is moving rapidly to focus using [Flex Spot: M], configure your focus area into [Zone] to much easier focus on individuals moving at greater speed.

Ice hockey

Recommended settings

Focus Area	[Flexible Spot: M] [Expand Flexible Spot]
Face/Eye AF Set.	Face/Eye Priority in AF: [Off]
Priority Set in AF-C	[Balanced Emphasis]
AF Track Sens	[4]
Swt. V/H AF Area	[AF Point Only]

Set Autofocus subjects-track sensitivity into the reasonably response level four provides better results if puck is passed rapidly from one player to the other.

If you are photographing many subjects near together or a subject that is more distant, configure the focus area to [Expand Flex Spot] instead of the suggested [Flex Spot: M].

Curling

Recommended settings

Focus Area	[Tracking: Flexible Spot M] [Flexible Spot: M] [Expand Flexible Spot]
Face/Eye AF Set.	Face/Eye Priority in AF: [On] Subject Detection: [Human]
Priority Set in AF-C	[Balanced Emphasis]
AF Track Sens	[2]
Swt. V/H AF Area	[AF Point Only]

- [Tracking: Flexible Spot M]

It is advised to choose [Tracking: Flex Spot M] when you wish to use the tracking feature to capture a particular subject, for example, when you are shooting straight ahead of the subject while they take a shot.

Focusing repeatedly on a particular individual, it is suggested that you configure [Eye/Face Priority in Autofocus] into [On] and utilize it in conjunction with your tracking function. Your camera automatically track eyes and faces when the individual's body is within the focus area and the face detection becomes available.

Tracking the individual, the framing may be changed based on your preference. It allows for modifications to the arrangement, like balancing backgrounds and other subjects inside the shot.

Holding your shutter button midway or utilizing Flexible Spot again is useful while quickly shooting several subjects in sequence. Assigning [Reg. Custom Shoots Set] or [Tracking On] (Set to

Autofocus Tracking and On) into the Custom button enables you to rapidly change your tracking function off or on.

- **[Expand Flexible Spot]/[Flexible Spot: M]**

For much steadier focus on scenarios where objects move in the subject's front in which you wish to focus, suggested setting is [Expand Flex Spot]/[Flex Spot: M].

Setting the Autofocus subject-tracking awareness to an equally static two for steadier tracking of particular player.

If you are photographing many subjects near together or a subject that is more distant, configure the focus area to [Expand Flex Spot] instead of the suggested [Flex Spot: M].

Motorcycling (i.e., on-road) Karting, Car racing

Recommended settings

Focus Area	[Flexible Spot: M] [Expand Flexible Spot] [Tracking: Flexible Spot M]
Face/Eye AF Set.	Face/Eye Priority in AF: [Off]
Priority Set in AF-C	[Balanced Emphasis]
AF Track Sens	[3 (Standard)]
Swt. V/H AF Area	[AF Point Only]

- **[Expand Flexible Spot]/[Flexible Spot: M]**

For much steadier focus on scenarios where objects move in the subject's front in which you wish to focus, suggested setting is [Zone] or [Flex Spot: M].

Autofocus subjects-track sensitivity setting three (Standard) enables stability tracking even while capturing motorsports with a lot of deceleration and acceleration.

The useful suggested setting for your focus area is your [Flex Spot: M], nevertheless, if the motorcycles or cars are farther, set to [Expand Flex Spot].

- **[Tracking: Flex Spot M]**

The recommended setting for tracking a particular motorcycle, car, and so on, for an individual shot is [Tracking: Flex Spot M]. when concentrating on particular subjects as a specific car or a formula car driver's helmet, [Flex Spot: M] works well. You can change the frame during tracking to suit your tastes. This makes compositional changes possible, such as balancing the automobiles and background in the shot.

The Motocross

Recommended settings

Focus Area	[Flexible Spot: M] [Wide] [Tracking: Wide]
Face/Eye AF Set.	Face/Eye Priority in AF: [Off]
Priority Set in AF-C	[Balanced Emphasis]
AF Track Sens	[3 (Standard)]
Swt. V/H AF Area	[AF Point Only]

- **[Wide]/[Flexible Spot: M]**

For aerial jump shots, use [Wide] and [Flex Spot: M] if the bikes are travelling in the ground. When shooting continuously, employ a broad focus area to change up the composition. If the AF locks on and the individual is on the screen's middle, with your focus area configured to [Wide], the subject may be tracked nearly full screen. this enables arrangement to be readily changed even when filming continuously.

- **[Tracking: Wide]**

Choose [Tracking: Wide] for easy capturing of the subject when it is advancing too quickly to line up with your focus area, for example, if the individual is mid-jump. You have the ability to change the framing while tracking to suit your tastes. This makes it possible to make compositional changes, like balancing the motorcycles as well as the background in the picture. It is advised to use [Tracking: Flex Spot M] while tracking a motorbike, and so forth for a single shot.

The Swimming

Recommended settings

Focus Area	[Expand Flexible Spot] [Flexible Spot: M]
Face/Eye AF Set.	Face/Eye Priority in AF: [On] Subject Detection: [Human]
Priority Set in AF-C	[Balanced Emphasis]
AF Track Sens	[1(Locked on)] to [2]
Swt. V/H AF Area	[AF Point Only]

Configure Autofocus subject-tracking awareness to one or two when capturing swimmers to evade the focus travelling into the background while they dive underneath the water. Utilize [Expand Flex Spot] to prevent focus from moving to the water's surface or splashing.

Cycle race

Recommended settings

Focus Area	[Flexible Spot: M] [Expand Flexible Spot] [Tracking: Flexible Spot M]
Face/Eye AF Set.	Face/Eye Priority in AF: [On] Subject Detection: [Human]
Priority Set in AF-C	[Balanced Emphasis]
AF Track Sens	[3 (Standard)]
Swt. V/H AF Area	[AF Point Only]

- **[Expand Flexible Spot]/[Flexible Spot: M]**

For much steadier focus on scenarios where numerous vehicles travelling as group, the suggested setting is [Expand Flex Spot] or Flex Spot: M].

Setting the Autofocus subject-tracking awareness to three (Standard) enables tracking steadier, with your focus less probable to change to other obstacles and subjects.

- **[Tracking: Flex Spot M]**

While capturing a single individual, it is advised that you configure your focus area into [Tracking: Flex Spot M], that enables more change in composition.

Focusing repeatedly on a particular individual, it is suggested that you configure [Eye/Face Priority in Autofocus] into [On] and utilize it in conjunction with your tracking function.

Your camera automatically track eyes and faces when the individual's body is within the focus area and the face detection becomes available. Tracking the individual, the framing may be changed based on your preference. It allows for modifications to the arrangement, like balancing backgrounds and other subjects inside the shot.

Horseracing Archery

Recommended settings

Focus Area	[Tracking: Flexible Spot M] [Flexible Spot: M] [Expand Flexible Spot]
Face/Eye AF Set.	Face/Eye Priority in AF: [On] Subject Detection: [Human]
Priority Set in AF-C	[Balanced Emphasis]
AF Track Sens	[3 (Standard)]
Swt. V/H AF Area	[AF Point Only]

- **[Tracking: Flex Spot M]**

Shooting a single subject, the suggested setting is [Flex Spot: M]. Focusing repeatedly on a particular individual, it is suggested that you configure [Eye/Face Priority in Autofocus] into [On] and utilize it in conjunction with your tracking function. Your camera automatically track eyes and faces when the individual's body is within the focus area and the face detection becomes available.

Tracking the individual, the framing may be changed based on your preference. It allows for modifications to the arrangement, like balancing backgrounds and other subjects inside the shot.

- **[Expand Flexible Spot]/[Flexible Spot: M]**

For much steadier focus on scenarios like shooting a horse racing pack, the suggested setting is [Expand Flex Spot] or Flex Spot: M]. Setting the Autofocus subject-tracking awareness to three (Standard) enables tracking steadier, with your focus less probable to change to other obstacles and subjects.

Speedboat racing

Focus Area	[Tracking: Flexible Spot M] [Flexible Spot: M] [Expand Flexible Spot]
Face/Eye AF Set.	Face/Eye Priority in AF: [Off]
Priority Set in AF-C	[Balanced Emphasis]
AF Track Sens	[3 (Standard)]
Swt. V/H AF Area	[AF Point Only]

- **The [Tracking: Flex Spot M]**

While shooting a particular boat, the suggested setting is [Flex Spot: M]. In some instances, for example, when an individual is putting on a helmet, face detection can be challenging. If your focus area shifts into a different face besides your subject's, turn [Eye/Face Priority in Autofocus] off.

- **[Expand Flexible Spot]/[Flex Spot: M]**

When you wish to track individual on the lead as subject's area constantly exchanging positions, like at the start of the race, it is suggested that you configure your focus area into [Expand Flex Spot] or [Flex Spot: M].

Setting the Autofocus subject-tracking awareness to three (Standard) enables tracking steadier, with your focus less probable to change to other obstacles and subjects.

Equestrian events, Canoeing

Recommended settings

Focus Area	[Flexible Spot: M] [Expand Flexible Spot] [Tracking: Flexible Spot M]
Face/Eye AF Set.	Face/Eye Priority in AF: [On] Subject Detection: [Human]
Priority Set in AF-C	[Balanced Emphasis]
AF Track Sens	[2]
Swt. V/H AF Area	[AF Point Only]

- **[Expand Flexible Spot]/[Flexible Spot: M]**

For much steadier focus on sports which include obstacles like equestrianism or canoeing, it is suggested that you configure your focus into [Expand Flex Spot] or [Flex Spot: M].

Setting the Autofocus subject-tracking awareness to three (Standard) enables tracking steadier, with your focus less probable to change to other obstacles and subjects.

- **[Tracking: Flex Spot M]**

If you wish to track particular individual, it is advised that you configure your focus area into [Tracking: Flex Spot M]. Focusing repeatedly on a particular individual, it is suggested that you configure [Eye/Face Priority in Autofocus] into [On] and utilize it in conjunction with your tracking function.

Your camera automatically track eyes and faces when the individual's body is within the focus area and the face detection becomes available. Tracking the individual, the framing may be changed based on your preference. It allows for modifications to the arrangement, like balancing backgrounds and other subjects inside the shot.

Holding your shutter button midway or utilizing Flexible Spot again is useful while quickly shooting several subjects in sequence.

Assigning [Reg. Custom Shoots Set] or [Tracking On] (Set to Autofocus Tracking and On) into the Custom button enables you to rapidly change your tracking function off or on.

Judo

Recommended settings

Focus Area	[Flexible Spot: M] [Expand Flexible Spot]
Face/Eye AF Set.	Face/Eye Priority in AF: [On] Subject Detection: [Human]
Priority Set in AF-C	[Balanced Emphasis]
AF Track Sens	[3 (Standard)]
Swt. V/H AF Area	[AF Point Only]

Effectiveness can be achieved with the flexible default suggested settings (focus area: [Flex Spot: M]; Autofocus subject-tracking awareness: Standard three). Try adjusting the sensor strength into the stronger two and your focus area into [Expand Flex Spot] when there are several barriers. Any eye or face that is detected within the specified focus area automatically will be monitored if [Eye/Face Priority in Autofocus] is configured to [On].

Kendo

Recommended settings

Focus Area	[Flexible Spot: M] [Expand Flexible Spot]
Face/Eye AF Set.	Face/Eye Priority in AF: [Off]
Priority Set in AF-C	[Balanced Emphasis]
AF Track Sens	[3 (Standard)]
Swt. V/H AF Area	[AF Point Only]

Effectiveness can be achieved with the flexible default suggested settings (focus area: [Flex Spot: M]; Autofocus subject-tracking awareness: Standard three). Try adjusting the sensor strength into the stronger two and your focus area into [Expand Flex Spot] when there are several barriers.

Face detection can be challenging in some occasions, like when an individual is putting on a protective gear. When your focus area shifts into a different face besides your subject's, turn [Eye/Face Priority in Autofocus] off.

Fencing

Recommended settings

Focus Area	[Flexible Spot: M] [Expand Flexible Spot] [Tracking: Flexible Spot M]
Face/Eye AF Set.	Face/Eye Priority in AF: [Off]
Priority Set in AF-C	[Balanced Emphasis]
AF Track Sens	[3 (Standard)]
Swt. V/H AF Area	[AF Point Only]

- **[Expand Flexible Spot]/[Flexible Spot: M]**

For much steadier focus on scenarios where objects move in the subject's front in which you wish to focus, suggested setting is [Expand Flex Spot]/[Flex Spot: M].

For much steadier focus on scenarios where individuals' movement are hard to guess and individuals tends to leave the focus area, configure the Autofocus subject-tracking awareness into the stronger two. Utilize [Expand Flex Spot] into focus on single subject.

- **[Tracking: Flex Spot M]**

If you wish to track particular individual, it is advised that you configure your focus area into [Tracking: Flex Spot M].

Face detection can be challenging in some occasions, like when an individual is putting on a protective gear. When your focus area shifts into a different face besides your subject's, turn [Eye/Face Priority in Autofocus] off.

271

Rhythmic gymnastics, gymnastics

Recommended settings

Focus Area	[Tracking: Flexible Spot M] [Flexible Spot: M] [Expand Flexible Spot]
Face/Eye AF Set.	Face/Eye Priority in AF: [On] Subject Detection: [Human]
Priority Set in AF-C	[Balanced Emphasis]
AF Track Sens	[3 (Standard)]
Swt. V/H AF Area	[AF Point Only]

- **[Tracking: Flex Spot M]**

If you wish to track an individual, like during single performance of the rhythmic gymnastics, you are therefore advised to configure your focus area into [Tracking: Flex Spot M]. Tracking function successfully enables you to easily change the composition in gymnastics.

Focusing repeatedly on a particular individual, it is suggested that you configure [Eye/Face Priority in Autofocus] into [On] and utilize it in conjunction with your tracking function.

Your camera automatically track eyes and faces when the individual's body is within the focus area and the face detection becomes available. Tracking the individual, the framing may be changed based on your preference. It allows for modifications to the arrangement, like balancing backgrounds and other subjects inside the shot.

- **[Expand Flexible Spot]/[Flexible Spot: M]**

If you wish to change the individual on which you want to focus, like while a team performs on rhythmic gymnastics, you are therefore advised to configure your focus area into [Expand Flex Spot] or [Flex Spot: M].

Configuring the Autofocus subject-tracking awareness into three (Standard) enables tracking to be more steadier, with focus less probable to move into the individual's hand or a pole.

Golf

Focus Area	[Tracking: Flexible Spot M] [Flexible Spot: M] [Expand Flexible Spot]
Face/Eye AF Set.	Face/Eye Priority in AF: [On] Subject Detection: [Human]
Priority Set in AF-C	[Balanced Emphasis]
AF Track Sens	[2]
Swt. V/H AF Area	[AF Point Only]

- **[Tracking: Flex Spot M]**

If you wish to track particular individual, it is advised that you configure your focus area into [Tracking: Flex Spot M]. Tracking the individual, the framing may be changed based on your preference. It allows for modifications to the arrangement, like balancing backgrounds and other subjects inside the shot.

Focusing repeatedly on a particular individual, it is suggested that you configure [Eye/Face Priority in Autofocus] into [On] and utilize it in conjunction with your tracking function.

Your camera automatically track eyes and faces when the individual's body is within the focus area and the face detection becomes available.

Face detection can be challenging in certain situations, like when an individual is putting on sunglasses. When your focus area adjusts to a different face besides your subject's, you are therefore advised to configure [Eye/Face Priority in Autofocus] to [Off].

- **[Expand Flexible Spot]/[Flex Spot: M]**

For much steadier focus on scenarios where objects move in the subject's front in which you wish to focus, suggested setting is [Expand Flex Spot]/[Flex Spot: M].

Setting the Autofocus subject-tracking awareness to a stronger two for steadier focus. The setting is suggested for shooting of bunker shots, if sand moves in the subject's front, and similar scenarios.

Other railed automobiles and Trains

Recommended settings

Focus Area	[Tracking: Flexible Spot M] [Flexible Spot: M] [Expand Flexible Spot]
Face/Eye AF Set.	Face/Eye Priority in AF: [Off]
Priority Set in AF-C	[Balanced Emphasis]
AF Track Sens	[3 (Standard)]
Swt. V/H AF Area	[AF Point Only]

- [Tracking: Flex Spot M]

If you wish to focus repeatedly on the very first vehicle of travelling train, the suggested setting is the [Tracking: Flex Spot M].

- **[Expand Flex Spot]/[Flex Spot: M]**

In the event when the composition is set before filming, shoot using your versatile fundamental suggested settings (Autofocus subject-tracking awareness: Standard three; focus area [Flex Spot: M]). If numerous obstructions, like overhead wiring are present, it is advised that you configure the Autofocus subject-tracking awareness into the spot-on [Expand Flex Spot].

The Wild birds

Recommended settings

Focus Area	[Flexible Spot: M] [Expand Flexible Spot] [Tracking: Wide]
Face/Eye AF Set.	Face/Eye Priority in AF: [Off]
Priority Set in AF-C	[Balanced Emphasis]
AF Track Sens	[3 (Standard)]
Swt. V/H AF Area	[AF Point Only]

- [Expand Flexible Spot]/[Flexible Spot: M]

Assuming that the subject may be filmed in the frame and that its' movement is known, configure the camera into the versatile fundamental suggested settings (Autofocus subject-tracking awareness: Standard three; focus area: [Flex Spot: M]). If numerous obstructions, it is advised that you configure the

Autofocus subject-tracking awareness into the stronger two and your focus area into the spot-on [Expand Flex Spot].

- **The [Tracking: Wide]**

It is advisable to configure your focus area into [Tracking: Wide] when capturing a situation where the target subject, like flying bird, is the only subject in the frame. If the bird moves quickly and makes framing problematic, using [Tracking: Wide] will make it easier to film the subject.

Air shows, Airplanes

Recommended settings

Focus Area	[Tracking: Flexible Spot M] [Flexible Spot: M] [Zone]
Face/Eye AF Set.	Face/Eye Priority in AF: [Off]
Priority Set in AF-C	[Balanced Emphasis]
AF Track Sens	[3 (Standard)]
Swt. V/H AF Area	[AF Point Only]

- **[Tracking: Flexible Spot M]**

It is advisable to configure your focus area into [Tracking: Flex Spot M]] when tracking a scenario where the target subject, is the only subject in the scene.

[Tracking: Flex Spot M] works well if you wish to keep your focu fixed on a specific aircraft. To make it easier to film the subject when photographing aerobatics as well as other scenes in which framing is a challenge, choose [Tracking: Wide].

- **[Zone]/[Flex Spot: M]**

For much steadier focus on scenarios where objects move in the subject's front in which you wish to focus, suggested setting is [Zone] or [Flex Spot: M].

Consider using the adaptable [Flex Spot: M] as your focus area setting. When framing is challenging, like when photographing airplanes flying acrobatics during an aerial show, use [Zone].

Wild animals

Recommended settings

Focus Area	[Flexible Spot: M] [Expand Flexible Spot] [Tracking: Flexible Spot M]
Face/Eye AF Set.	Face/Eye Priority in AF: [On] Subject Detection: [Animal]
Priority Set in AF-C	[Balanced Emphasis]
AF Track Sens	[2]
Swt. V/H AF Area	[AF Point Only]

- **[Expand Flexible Spot]/[Flexible Spot: M]**

For much steadier focus on scenarios where objects move in the subject's front in which you wish to focus, suggested setting is [Zone] or [Flex Spot: M].

[Expand Flex Spot] is advise in environments having obstructions such as branches and bushes.

- **[Tracking: Flexible Spot M]**

It is advisable to configure your focus area into [Tracking: Flex Spot M]] when tracking a scenario where the target subject, is the only subject in the scene.

Focusing repeatedly on a particular individual, it is suggested that you configure [Eye/Face Priority in Autofocus] into [On] and utilize it in conjunction with your tracking function. Your camera automatically track eyes and faces when the individual's body is within the focus area and the face detection becomes available. Tracking the individual, the framing may be changed based on your preference.

Shooting Tips

Choose Focus Area on the basis of the individual size on the screen

Determine the approximate dimensions of your Focus Area, like Flexible Spot, based on the subject's screen size.

The photo should be broad enough to cover the entire Focus Area for the Flexible Spot. By keeping the photo at a size like this, the photo is kept from going into the background.

When using Expand Flex Spot, the topic as well Focus Area should almost entirely overlap.

For a given skating scene, the ideal Focus Area dimension is determined by the size of the topic on screen.

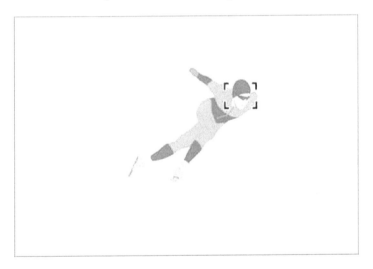

It is advised to focus on the individual's face using Flex Spot M. If Zone is configured, the camera may focus on rink line markers or other items that are within the designated area rather than the skater.

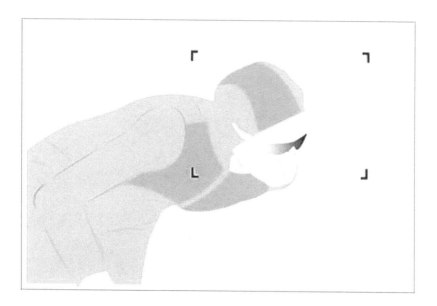

Try a broader option like Zone if you want to use a lengthy focal length to capture a moving person at this scale. Select [Autofocus Point Only] for switching Horizontal and Vertical Autofocus Area if you need to alternate between holding your camera horizontally and vertically. Although ice hockey and American football seem to require similar environments, there are a few minor variations on how to shoot each of them more effectively.

Expand Flex Spot can more precisely locate the subject in sports like rugby and American football where players collide.

If the individual is moving quickly, such as in ice hockey, attempt to keep your Focus Area similar size as the player (N in the above example). The camera might not concentrate on the correct player if there are too many in a big area.

Choose Focus Area on the basis of the subject movement

Small-area environment such as Expand Flex Spot will locate the target point precisely if the individual is moving steadily or slowly. Wide, or broader Focus Area, keeps focus while enabling you to make compositional adjustments when an individual is moving quickly or erratically.

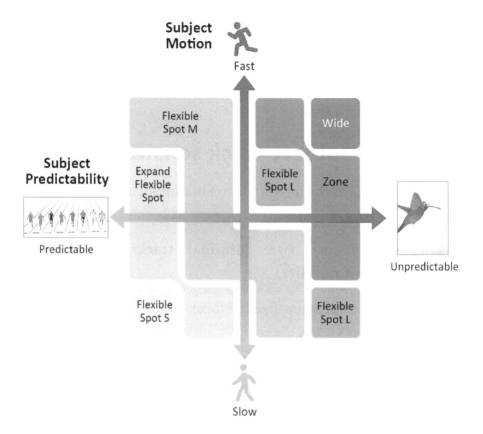

- If your Focus area is configured into [Zone] or [Wide] in the Autofocus control setting:
  - ⊡ [Wide]: Therefore, we advise putting your subject near or at the middle of your screen prior to focusing.
  - ⊡ [Zone]: Therefore, we advise putting your subject near or at the middle of your zone area prior to focusing.

    With [Zone] and [Wide], immediately your focus is verified and your focus symbol ◉ is illuminated, the individual will stay in the focus inside the focusing region, giving you more compositional freedom.

- Flex Spot S works well for focusing in a very small region, nevertheless, it may be challenging to concentrate on particular topics. Expand Flex Spot auto focuses in your expanded region when the camera is unable to focus within the S-shaped area.

Autofocus subject-track sensitivity

There are 5 stages of the focus tracking in Autofocus Control Focus Mode.

1 (Locked on) into two: Minimal tracking sensitivity (concentrates on stability)

The chosen subject remains fixed in focus and in a stable posture.

Four to five (Responsive): Extreme tracking sensitivity (concentrates on responsiveness)

As opposed to tracking one subject, the camera swiftly focuses on objects that are close by.

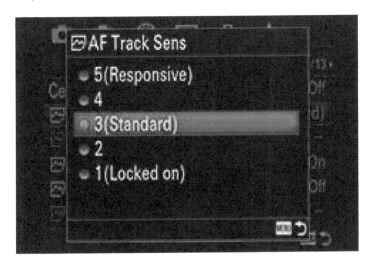

As a general reference, the settings have to be two while tracking a particular player in sport such as American football in which the players are colliding with one another, or three (standard) when an individual is passing the subject's front.

In soccer, players are basically far away from each other so four is the best settings since it concentrates more on responsiveness rather than lock-on. If adjusted to four, the focus won't move to a different player when their entire body obstruct the initial subject.

AF-C's Priority Set

To get a nice balance between release settings and existing Autofocus, try using Balanced Emphasis. Useful for combining precise focus control with seizing an important moment when filming moving objects.

The AF

Before your subject comes into focus, the shutter can't be released. When using this setting, concentration should take precedence over continuous shooting speed.

(Based on the scenario, your constant shooting speed can become slower or your shooting interval can become uneven.)

The Release

You can take pictures at any moment with this setting, but you run the chance of taking a lot of out-of-focus shots. It helps keep continuous shooting at a steady pace.

The Balanced Emphasis

When employing [Release], the individual is more probable to be on focus. Compared to utilizing [Release], your continuous shooting pace will be marginally slower. This option is advised for taking pictures of moving objects since the camera chooses the shooting strategy just prior to the shutter release time. When timing matters more, utilize [Release].

Comparing Release and Balanced Emphasis

Release has the benefit of maintaining Continuous Shooting time even when the individual moves around a lot. It's helpful when filming a movie or taking a bunch of continuous shots. For instance, consider taking a picture of a soccer player striking the ball. The kick may go unnoticed by AF, but all of the photos taken by Release might not be in focus. Some useful photos will be provided by Balanced Emphasis.

Switch Horizontal and Vertical AF Area

Select whether to change the Focus Area options and focusing frame position to match the vertical/horizontal orientation of the camera. Although [Off] is the standard setting, it is advised to use [Autofocus Point Only] if you often reorient the camera, for example, vertically if the subject comes nearer.

[Off]

[Autofocus Point Only]

[Focus Area + AF Point]

The Silent Shooting

Recommended settings

Shutter Type	Electronic Shut.
Audio signals	Off

Mechanical Shutter generates shutter noise, that can be challenging in conditions that need silence. Since Electronic Shutter makes no vibration or sound, it is helpful for the silent shooting. Shutdown only occurs during Continuous Shooting if the Audio notifications are disabled and Shutter Type has been configured to Auto. Each Drive Modes become silent if the Shutter Type has been configured to Electronic Shutter.

Other

Autofocus Area Registration Operation allows you reg. your Focus Area using Autofocus On into a custom button (AF On + Reg. AF Area) so you can immediately change to it. For instance, when you normally configure Flex Spot M, nevertheless, the individual comes closer or leaves your focusing frame, you may click the customized button to activate AF utilizing the reg. Focus Area.

If the targeted subjects are detected on your screen, put the flex spot in the face that you wish to focus, and then click the Eye Autofocus key to focus more on the desired individual's eyes.

Tracking Subjects

To track subject (The tracking function)

Configure the individual by clicking your shutter button midway down to enable the camera auto track the individual. In addition, focusing frame effortlessly moves between the subject's eyes and face whether it is a human, based on the subject's situation.

Configuring the start point to track via focusing area

The Tracking begins by utilizing your focus frame on [Tracking] option on [Focus Area] to be the start position. Aiming at your setting & subject [Tracking] will help you target a specific area or improve your odds of filming a moving subject.

You should configure [Tracking] into [Expand Flex Spot] or [Flex Spot M] if there are several athletes or if the individual is small. The athlete will remain the center of focus when you begin tracking, unaffected by other subjects.

Configure [Tracking] to [Wide] or [Zone] if you wish to track subject which is moving rapidly and there aren't any other subjects nearby. This makes it easy to film the subject and reduces the chance of the focus moving into the background.

Connection between [Eye/Face AF Set] and Tracking.

When you configure [Eye/Face Priority on Autofocus] to concentrate on eyes/faces beforehand, focusing frame auto display around a verified eye or face during subject tracking.

Modifying your setting for [The Focus Area] into [Tracking] temporarily

Temporarily tracking the subject (Tracking On)

While you tap and hold the custom button that you have pre-assigned [Tracking On], you may temporarily switch your [Focus Area] setting to [Tracking]. The [Tracking] setting will replace your [Focus Area] configuration that was in place before you turned on [Tracking On].

For example:

[Focus Area] before you activate [Tracking On]	[Focus Area] while [Tracking On] is active
[Wide]	[Tracking: Wide]
[Flexible Spot: S]	[Tracking: Flexible Spot S]
[Expand Flexible Spot]	[Tracking: Expand Flexible Spot]

Conditions where by [Tracking On] becomes useful

To track when the intended subject is obscured by an obstacle or the subject is small

1. Track using [Flex Spot] if the intended subject is obscured by an obstacle or the intended subject is small and farther away

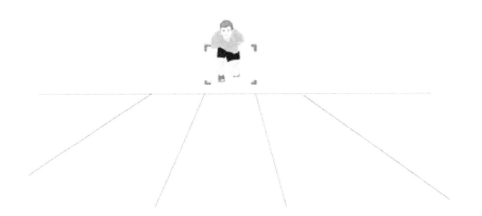

2. If the aimed athlete comes nearer, hold the shutter button and held midway down and click [Tracking On]

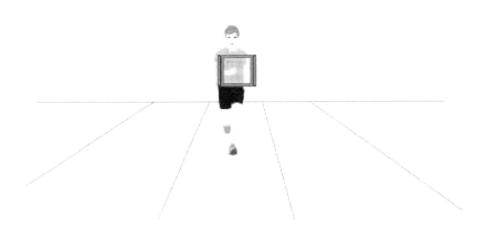

3. Also, you may change the composition while tracking

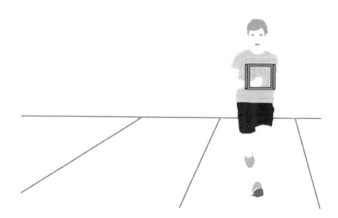

Stop track and then tracking a subject using [Flex Spot]

1. Configure [Flex Spot] point to the place that is easier to film the subject. Holding down the custom key designated as [Tracking On], track A.

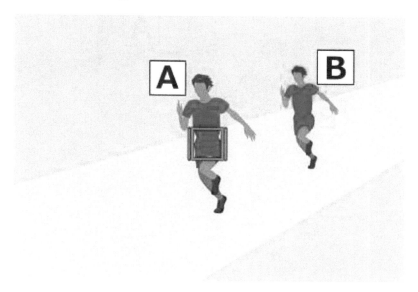

2. To modify the tracking focus subject into B

3. Let go of Tracking On customized button & track B using [Flex Spot] which was previously configured. You may change between [Flex Spot] and [Tracking] as desired.

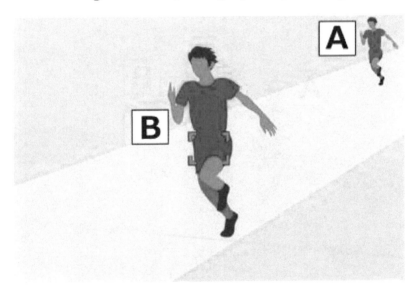

Connection between [Eye/Face AF Set] and Tracking.

When you configure [Eye/Face Priority on Autofocus] to concentrate on eyes/faces beforehand, focusing frame auto display around a verified eye or face during subject tracking.

Changing your tracking function off & on while utilizing your flex spot (Registration Custom Shoot Set)

It is advised that you choose the flexible location for your focus area when you wish to swiftly swap between subjects while autofocusing. But, using your flex spot in conjunction with tracking is helpful when photographing a subject moving quickly and in a freely constructed shot. For easier swapping between functions, assign your tracking function into a button that is readily accessible, like your Autofocus-ON button. You may focus using your flex spot by pressing your shutter button midway down. The subject is tracked when your Autofocus-ON button is pressed.

Operating process

From MENU to **■2** (Camera Settings two), to [🖉 Cust Key], then move to [Autofocus-ON Button], move to [Recall Cust hold one], move to Configure [Focus Mode] into [Autofocus-Control], [Focus Area] into [Tracking: Flex Spot M], plus [Autofocus On] into [On].

- The [Focus Mode]: [Autofocus-Control]
- [Focus Area]: [Flexi Spot: M]

Instances of scenarios where alternating between [Recall Cust hold] and [Flex Spot] works well.

Use your flex spot to capture images of multiple subjects. Click your Autofocus-ON key to begin tracking when there is just a single subject or when the individual is moving quickly.

Immediately after the marathon begins, at the time when the runners are continually swapping places, capture each runner using your flex spot function.

During the last lap, utilize your Autofocus-ON button's tracking function to capture a particular runner in the ideal composition, paying focus to how the background & subject balance out.

To Focus on An Individual's Eyes Or Face

To take pictures of someone by focusing on their eye or face, adopt the following technique. Two different shooting techniques exist. Utilize whichever approach is appropriate for the shooting situation. Additionally, you can choose to identify the right or left eye.

Note:

Install the most recent version of the system software on the camera.

1. While shooting pictures by holding your shutter button midway down. Alternatively, by holding your Autofocus-ON (Autofocus On) button

Core usages

- If you wish to capture an image with a complicated composition but still want your camera to concentrate on the targeted subject, like when you want to capture the light in a particular person's eye.
- When you wish to keep focusing utilizing [Focus Area] just in case it's difficult to detect an eye but want to concentrate on the subject that has a higher importance in the eye.

2. When capturing pictures by transferring [Eye Autofocus] into a custom button

Core usages

- If you wish to depend on your camera function, independent of the [Focus Area] setting, to momentarily focus on a particular eye anywhere in the monitor's viewing area.

1. When capturing pictures by holding your shutter button midway down. Alternatively, by holding your Autofocus-ON (Autofocus On) button

Suggested scenes

- Shooting multiple people when you wish to concentrate on a particular person's face (or eye) out of two or multiple people on the screen. photographing sports events or other scenes where erratic movements frequently make it challenging to identify the eyes. When the camera is unable to concentrate on an eye or face, it will focus on the person on your focus area. Without missing your shutter chance, you can take the picture.

Core features

- You may choose a setting for the [Focus Area]. ([Flex Spot], [Zone], [Wide], etc.)
- Focusing on a single eye is possible if your focus area crosses over onto a face (facial detection frame). Both the eye and the face can be focused on when your focus area and facial detection frames overlap. Under [Autofocus-Control] focus mode settings. Focusing on a person's face takes place if the camera cannot identify an eye.
- Focusing on the subject within your focus area occurs when it doesn't overlap the facial detection frame. (The standard autofocus procedure is executed.)

Operating process

Choose MENU, click ▣1 (Camera Settings one), click [Eye/Face AF Set.], click on [Eye/Face Priority in AF], then click [On].

Choose MENU click ▣1 (Camera Settings one), click [Eye/Face AF Set.], click on [Subject Detection], then click [Human]. Choose the preferred configuration items for [Eye/Face Frame Display] & [Left/Right Eye Select].

If eyes are identified: Concentrates on the eyes

If eyes aren't identified: Tracks making use of the configured [Focus Area]

The [Focus Area] configurations

You may concentrate on either eye or face when focus area and facial detection frames coincide. In this manner, you can change to the optimal focus area based on the scene being shot. For instance, the facial detection frame turns from gray into white when [Flex Spot] of the [Focus Area] overlaps it, allowing you to concentrate on either eye or face. Your eye detection frames occurs when [Left/Right Eye Select] isn't configured to [Auto]. Alternatively, when you use your custom button to execute [Switch Left/Right Eye]

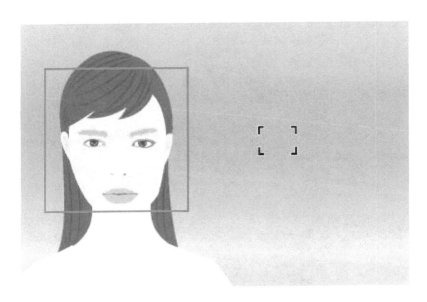

Eye and face are out of focus

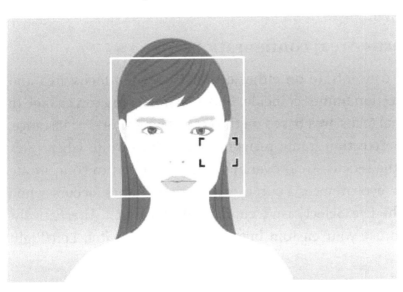

Able to focus on an eye or face

- **[Wide]**: Ideal for subjects which are in motion or when faces are in unusual positions.

- **[Expand Flex Spot] [Flex Spot], [Center], [Zone]:** Set a time to focus in a particular subject among several, or select beforehand how to arrange photos.

Connection between [Eye/Face AF Set] & Tracking.

When you configure [Eye/Face Priority on Autofocus] to concentrate on eyes/faces beforehand, focusing frame auto display around a verified eye or face during subject tracking.

This works well for taking sports photos, portraits of models spinning, and other similar scenarios.

1. Tracking far-off subjects

2. When the person gets closer and the person's face is identified, your focusing frame moves to the eyes or face

This enables you to take pictures in situations when it would normally be challenging to focus in the eyes.

When an eye-blocking object, such as gymnastic ribbon, is present

Timing a forward-facing athlete during a crouched start

To time a fighter who is facing front

2. When capturing pictures by transferring [Eye Autofocus] into a custom button

Utilize your Eye Autofocus function by transferring [Eye Autofocus] into a custom button. The camera may focus in the person's eyes so far you are clicking this custom button.

Suggested scenes

- Shooting a moving person or a portraits
- Whenever you wish to capture a person with eye priority for focus.
- In order to get a good picture of someone, you should focus first on their eyes. No matter how big or where your focus area is, the camera recognizes a face immediately as it comes into the monitor's field of view and locks onto one of the eyes. You may utilize [Eye Autofocus] without adjusting your [Focus Area] option, for instance, if you wish to focus in an eye beyond your focus frame if [Focus Area] has been configured into [Flex Spot]. So long as you rely on the function of the camera, you may capture even moving subject.

Core features

- You are unable to choose another setting for the [Focus Area]; if it is currently configured to [Wide]. If you wish to temporarily employ your Eye Autofocus function across the entire monitor, this function comes in handy.
- No matter where the subject (human) displays on the screen, your camera recognizes an eye or a face to focus

upon. So long as the custom button designated for [Eye Autofocus] is held won, your camera recognizes and focus on any eyes within the monitor's viewing range. (While using [Autofocus-Control] as your focus mode).

- The focusing feature is deactivated when your camera cannot identify an eye or a face

Operating process

1. Choose MENU, click 1 (Camera Settings one), click on [Eye/Face AF Set.], click on [Subject Detection], then click on [Human].
   Choose the preferred configuration items for [Eye/Face Frame Display] and.

2. Choose MENU, click on 2 (Camera Settings two), click on [Custom Key], click on the desired key, and then designate your [Eye Autofocus] function into the key.

3. When the camera is aimed at someone's face, hit the key designated for your [Eye Autofocus] function.

4. While holding down the key, tap your shutter button.

If eyes are identified: Concentrates on the eyes

If eyes aren't identified: Doesn't focus. Suggested for conditions like portrait capturing where you wish to constantly focus on just the eyes

Indicates the eye that has to be found. [Choose Left/Right Eye]

Not only can you choose which eye to automatically focus on, but you can also choose the left or right eye beforehand. For instance, you can focus on shooting and composition when the intended eye has been identified when taking a portrait. You can select [Auto], [Left Eye], or [Right Eye] from the [Left/Right Eye Select] menu in your menu.

When utilizing Eye AF for photography, the setting will be shown. Additionally, you can quickly switch between [Left Eye] & [Right Eye] while shooting by pressing your custom key assigned to [Switch Left/Right Eye]. You can utilize this as the scene dictates.

Utilize Menu to choose which eyes to recognize

Operating process

Select MENU, click on 📷1 (Camera Settings one), click on [Eye/Face AF Set.], click on [Left/Right Eye Select], then click on preferred setting item.

- **The [Auto]:** Eyes are automatically detected by the camera.
- **The [Right Eye]:** It is possible to identify the subject' right eye, which is also the left eye from the cameraman's point of view.
- **The [Left Eye]:** It is possible to identify the subject's left eye, which is also it right eye from the cameraman's point of view.

Switch among the right & left eye with every tap of the custom key

Operating process

Select MENU, click on 📷2 (Camera Settings two), click on [🖼 Custom Key], click on the preferred key, and then designate the [Switch Left/Right Eye] function into the button.

1. **When [Left/Right Eye Select] has been configured to [Left Eye] or [Right Eye]:**

You may switch among identifying the right or left eye with every tap of your custom button to which you've designate [Switch Left/Right Eye].

2. **When [Left/Right Eye Select] has been configured to [Auto]:**

You may utilize your custom button to which you've designate [Switch Left/Right Eye] can use the custom key to which you have assigned [Switch Right/Left Eye] to momentarily switch among the right or left eye.

The momentary right/left collection is deleted if you do the below operations, etc. Your camera goes back to auto eye detection.

- Pushing your shutter button, halfway.
- Ceasing to hit the designated custom key, [Eye AF] or [AF On].
- Tapping MENU button or Fn button.

To focus on the Eye of an animal

To take pictures of an animal by focusing on its eye, adopt the following technique. Two different shooting techniques exist, similar to the technique utilized for focusing in an eye or face of an individual.
Utilize either shooting technique based on the shooting circumstances determined by the two techniques.

1. Shooting pictures by holding your shutter button midway down. Alternatively, pressing your AF-ON (Autofocus On) button

Determines whether to focus in the eyes of the animal if autofocus is engaged and if it recognizes the eye of the animal within your focusing area. In cases where the camera is unable to identify the eye of an animal, you can utilize the standard autofocus mode to modify the focus based on the chosen focus frame.

To set the camera

Utilize settings into focusing in the eye of the animal.

1. Choose MENU, click on 1 (Camera Settings one), click on [Eye/Face AF Set.], click on [Eye/Face Priority in AF], and then click [On].

2. Choose MENU, click on 1 (Camera Settings one), click on [Eye/Face AF Set.], click on [Subject Detection], and then click on [Animal].

3. Choose MENU, click on 1 (Camera Settings one), click on [Eye/Face AF Set.], click on [Animal Eyes Display], then click on the preferred setting.
    IF [On] is configured, white eye recognition frame displays around the eye.

Configure your [Focus Area] into [Wide] when you wish to recognize an eye at the widest possible range, given the camera is focused on the eye of the animal on your focus area.

Use [Zone] or [Flex Spot] as your [Focus Area] settings to restrict the range for eye detection.

Moreover, Focus Mode must be adjusted to Autofocus.

1. Choose MENU, click on 📷1 (Camera Settings one), click on [Focus Area], then click on the preferred setting.
2. Select Focus Mode, click on Autofocus-Single (Single-shot Autofocus). Alternatively, click on Continuous AF (AF-C).

To shoot still pictures

1. Aim the camera to capture the eye of the animal within the designated focus area.

If [Focus Area] has been configured to [Zone]

2. Hold your shutter button midway down. Alternatively, tap your AF-ON (Autofocus On) key to focus in the eye of the animal.

   Green eye recognition frame appears around the eye immediately the eye of the animal is recognized and the focusing is executed.

3. Hold your shutter button down fully.

Note:

- If you wish to change your [Subject Detection] option more easily, register your [Subject Detection] option to your Function menu. Alternatively, you can designate it to the Custom key.

- When an animal's face is small or there are multiple animals visible on your screen, you may choose to focus at just the animal's eye by setting [Focus Area] into [Flexible Spot].

This will make it simpler for your camera to identify the animal's eye when you focus on your subject.

Notice

- Your camera won't be capable of detecting an eye based on the shooting environment or subject.

Connection between [Eye/Face AF Set] and Tracking

When you configure [Eye/Face Prty in AF] into focusing on eyes in advance, focusing frame automatically will display over any recognized eye during subject tracking.

1. To track far away subjects

2. If the eye of an animal is recognized when the animal comes nearer, focusing frame automatically will display over the recognized eye.

2. Shooting pictures by designating [Eye AF] into the custom key

You may utilize the Eye Autofocus function key designating custom key for [Eye AF]. For as long you continue to hold down the key, the camera will lock on the eye of the animal. This is helpful if you wish to temporarily enable the Eye Autofocus function on the whole screen, independent of the [Focus Area] option.

To focus at an eye beyond your focusing frame, for example, when [Focus Area] has been configured to [Flexible Spot], you can use the Eye Autofocus function without adjusting [Focus Area] by hitting the custom button assigned to [Eye AF].

To set the camera

Utilize settings into focusing in the eye of the animal.

1. Choose MENU, click on 1 (Camera Settings one), click on [Eye/Face AF Set.], click on [Subject Detection], and then click on [Animal].

2. Choose MENU, click on 1 (Camera Settings one), click on [Eye/Face AF Set.], click on [Animal Eyes Display], then click on the preferred setting.
    IF [On] is configured, white eye recognition frame displays around the eye.

3. Choose MENU, click on 2 (Camera Settings two), click on [Custom Key]. And then, designate [Eye Autofocus] to the button you wish to utilize for the particular function on your selection screen.

Also, it is important to configure Focus Mode into Autofocus mode.

1. Select Focus Mode, click on Autofocus-Single (Single-shot Autofocus). Alternatively, select Continuous AF (AF-C).

To shoot still pictures

1. Hold your Custom button to the place where the [Eye Autofocus] function is designated.
   Green eye recognition frame appears around the eye immediately the eye of the animal is recognized and the focusing is executed.

2. Tap your shutter button as you holding your Custom Key down.

Note

If you wish to change your [Subject Detection] option more easily, register your [Subject Detection] option to your Function menu. Alternatively, you can designate it to the Custom key.

Notice

- Your camera won't be capable of detecting an eye based on the shooting environment or subject.

All you need to know about the Eye Detection

The camera may identify an eye with ease if the subjects have faces resembling those of cats or dogs and their eyes are easily identifiable. However, based on the kind of animal and the shooting conditions (e.g., multiple moving animals), the camera might not be capable of detecting an eye.

As a guide, consider the following instances.

Instances of the easy-to-detects animal's eye

Cat-like face

Dog-like face

The full face's size is sufficiently large enough to be easily seen

The face of the animal is oriented so that you can see its eyes & nose well

Instance of the difficult-to-detects animal's eye

The focus animal has striped/spotted body & face

While filming animals having dark hair or filming in dark areas

Animals that don't have dog or cat like faces

When there are multiple animals circling around

Tip

- The camera might not pick up the animal's eye if its face is not in focus. If so, shift the focus to the face just once. The camera may then identify the eye with more ease. After that, the camera can detect the eye more easily.

Made in United States
Troutdale, OR
03/14/2024